". . . AND YOU VISITED ME."

by Dennis E. Saylor

Director of Chaplaincy Services
Presbyterian Hospital Center
Albuquerque, New Mexico

PUBLISHED BY

MORSE PRESS, INC.

TM 417 East Pine St. • Seattle, WA 98122

"Since 1945"

COPYRIGHT, 1979 MORSE PRESS, INC.

Library of Congress Catalog Card
No. 79-88403

ISBN 0-93350-21-x

Printed in the USA

To Helen

TABLE OF CONTENTS

i

ACKNOWLEDGEMENTS

The writer is deeply indebted to Warren A. Heffron, M.D., A. Adams Lovekin, PhD., and Richard L. Lueker, M.D. for their able assistance in the preparation of this work. Each of these men read the manuscript and offered valuable suggestions. Their help is hereby acknowledged and appreciated.

To the medical librarians of Presbyterian Hospital, Mrs. Frances Szeman and Mrs. Helen Saylor, I am grateful for their aid in supplying reference material.

The typing of the several drafts of the manuscript was the work of Ms. Gretchen Otto, whose competent help was indispensable in its production. The encouragement and support of Richard R. Barr, Administrator, and Robert Shafer, Assistant Administrator of Presbyterian Hospital is acknowledged with gratitude.

Overview

Clergymen sometimes feel uncomfortable when visiting their parishioners who are hospitalized. In some instances, a pastor develops a reluctance which results in ineffective and infrequent hospital visits. Part of this reluctance stems from the fact that many theological seminaries do not offer specific training in hospital visitation, per se. Further, many pastors and seminarians do not have access to accredited programs of Clinical Pastoral Education. Even pastors who are trained in special counseling skills often do not fully appreciate the profound effect that hospitalization and specific medical problems have on the counseling situation.

Especially in smaller rural communities, opportunities for continuing education and supervised counseling experience are very limited. In the state of New Mexico, for example, there are no resident theological seminaries of any church group which offer continuing education courses in parish ministry. Only one hospital in the state provides any supervised clinical training. However, at least two schools of theology offer an advanced degree program on a non-resident basis.

Thus the lack of specific seminary training and limited access to continuing education opportunities make a written manual or book devoted to pastoral counseling in the hospital a significant contribution to the field. Further, it enables pastors whose personal schedule makes it virtually impossible to take advantage of accessible educational opportunities to avail themselves of additional insightful information. Also, a distillation of specific pastoral counseling skills useful in hospital visitation will help fill a void in the pastoral care literature.

In each of the following chapters, an attempt is made to integrate current psychological and counseling technique with the theological, environmental, and medical issues which confront the pastoral counselor. While no single counseling technique is propounded, an eclectic approach with a distinct Rogerian emphasis is implicit in this presentation.

The purpose of this study, then, is to develop such a manual that will meet the need for many parish pastoral counselors of all denominations. An ecumenical approach is essential and will be maintained throughout. The focus of the study will be three-fold: (1) the theological and philosophic foundations of pastoral care, (2) the influence of environmental factors on pastoral counseling, and (3) some specific counseling situations.

The theological and philosophic foundations of pastoral care is necessary to provide the justification of pastoral care in a medical facility. In order to do this an examination of various relational concepts is required. Since the practice of medicine is based entirely on the scientific method of inquiry and pastoral counseling has a distinct theological bias which is not based on scientific methodology, the appropriateness of such a service is a major issue. The first chapter, therefore, is a polemic defense or apologetic of the relationship of medicine and religion in terms of their respective epistomologies and the effect each has on health and wholeness.

The second chapter is devoted to the relationship of human sin and physical illness. This issue stems from pagan shamanism and reaches into the role of the pastoral counselor as a therapeutic agent. The whole area of the effect of the psychogenic factors in sickness is implied and approached from a Biblical perspective. Related to this but still distinct is the dilemma of human suffering. In actuality, this is the age-old theological problem of evil's existence in a universe created by a good God. The third chapter explores this question because the pastoral counselor faces this question in some form literally every day. As with the preceding chapter, Biblical exposition forms the basis for dealing with this theme.

A practical approach to the religious needs and various creeds of the patients he will visit is mandatory for the pastoral counselor. Therefore, a treatment of these areas are included in the fourth chapter. A general listing of the distinctive beliefs of the major religious groups on such subjects as baptism, the sacraments, and ritualistic ceremonies for Protestant, Roman Catholic and Jewish patients is necessary.

Chapter five deals with the topic of spiritual therapy. The distinctive role of the pastoral counselor is delineated. Also included in this chapter is a treatment of the appropriate use of Scripture and prayer, with illustrations of both. Some specific practical suggestions for visiting in the hospital are listed for consideration also.

The last chapter in this section, chapter six, touches on a special area of moral judgment. Taking the controversial question of the right to die, the moral and ethical considerations are carefully examined. A concrete description of what is referred to as the "quality of life" will be suggested with clinical examples. This chapter employs the perspective of the theological and philosophic foundations which are both implicit and explicit in the previous five chapters of the first major section of the book.

The second main topic will deal with the pastoral counselor and the impact of environmental factors on the hospitalized patient. The discussion begins with chapter seven and with an examination of the kinds, causes and implications of perception disorders which the pastoral counselor will encounter. Too often these patients are ignored and ministry to them is minimized. This is true not only of the geriatric patient but of patients of all other chronological ages.

The second chapter in the area of environmental impact, chapter eight, deals with hospital patients' perception of the hospitalization process from admission through discharge. It is very necessary for the pastoral counselor to know something of the perceptual field of the persons to whom he ministers. This treatment shows what losses the patient perceives attendant to hospitalization, his perceptions of the hospital staff and also his perceptions of hospital policy. It is the framework in which the pastoral counseling session is set and is of great importance that the pastoral counselor be aware of and appreciate it.

Chapter nine delves into the relationship of the pastoral counselor himself and the hospital staff. Two main topics are included in this: (1) the relationship of the pastoral counselor and the physician, and (2) his relationship with the nursing staff. This is extremely important to the pastoral counselor whose ministry is greatly enhanced by a relationship characterized by mutual respect and trust of the principals who relate so intimately to the same hospital population.

The tenth chapter explores the problem patients that are part and product of the hospital environment. Attention is given to the hostile patient, the manipulative patient and the self-destructive patient. A case history approach is utilized to illustrate intervention strategy. The pastoral counselor needs to be alert to the reasons for problem patient behavior, and how he can respond appropriately.

The first chapter in section three, as mentioned above, is chapter eleven which involves counseling with mothers of stillborn babies. The pastoral counselor needs to know how to handle his own feelings about death and the seeming unjust death of the newborn. Knowledge of how to relate to the mother at this time of great sensitivity is extremely important. This chapter uses the fives stages of grief suggested by Dr. Kubler-Ross and relates these to the counseling with the mothers of the stillborn.

The second chapter in this series presents the elements of counseling with the pre-surgical patient. The etiology of pre-surgical anxiety is examined and representative case histories are seen in the perspective of a possible model. Attention is given the role which the pastoral counselor plays in relieving such anxiety. Since a good portion of all hospital admissions are for some type of surgery, this is a necessary overview.

Chapter thirteen deals with a non-surgical patient (initially at least) of a classic genre. This is the cardiac patient. Pastoral counseling with this type of patient presents a unique challenge since there is such heightened emotionality about heart disease. Its prevalence in our society makes this an extremely relevant topic.

Like heart disease, cancer is a leading cause of death in the U.S. and is feared perhaps more than any other malady. No discussion of pastoral counseling would be complete without an extensive treatment of working with the cancer patient. In this chapter, Chapter fourteen, the varied stages of the disease will be examined along with attendant therapies, with particular attention given to the spiritual and religious resources along with family support the patient might have.

The fifteenth chapter is devoted to the orthopedic patient and how the pastoral counselor can be of help to him. Particular aspects such as chronic pain phenomena are noted as they apply to the counseling situation. Since most orthopedic patients are in the hospital longer than other types of patients, the quality of the rapport is important also.

While not all hospitals have a psychiatric unit, the pastoral counselor will encounter psychiatrically depressed patients and needs to understand some of the dynamics of depression. This chapter, sixteen, explains what depression is, how it is expressed, and what is the role of the pastoral counselor.

The seventeenth chapter of the book is a consideration of the terminal patient. Death and dying are being discussed at all levels openly. Specific topics covered in this chapter are anticipatory grief, unresolved conflicts and religious anxiety. These areas are of greatest concern to the pastoral counselor in his ministry.

As life expectancy increases, so does the number of older persons in our population. Their spiritual needs are addressed in chapter eighteen. Many hospitals are adding skilled nursing facilities and the number of nursing homes continues to increase. The whole area of geriatic care is just beginning to attract the national attention it merits.

The final chapter of this section and of the book is a brief look at wholistic health. As the interrelationship between body, mind and spirit becomes more apparent, the relationship between physical medicine and faith healing demands more scrutiny. This discussion offers a rational, yet spiritual, approach to healing.

These then are the chapters and topics which will be discussed in some detail using supportive research.

SECTION ONE

Theological and Philosophical Fields

Chapter I

Science, Religion, and Health

In arriving at a theological and philosophic foundation of pastoral care in the hospital setting, the pastoral counselor must acknowledge the unique relationship between medicine and religion. Further, the relationship must be resolved in such a way that it satisfies his own religious convictions and, at the same time, does not compromise his professional respect for the discipline of medicine. The question to be raised is whether the hospital is the exclusive domain of physical medicine or if one trained in a discipline based on entirely different philosophic premises can compatibly function in close relation, even cooperation. This is a basic and fundamental issue which must be faced with honesty and objectivity by all concerned.

It is historically interesting and important to note that many hospitals in the U.S. were founded by church groups or religious orders as were many institutions of higher learning. In fact, while it may be argued that in ancient Rome the temples of Aesculapius, the surgical dispensaries or iatria and the military valetudinaria pre-date the Christian era, one of the first hospitals in the West was founded by a wealthy Roman widow, Fabiola, in 390 A.D. (Marty, 1971).

To be sure, the care of the sick has been undertaken since the dawn of civilization. One of the earliest recorded references to sickness is in the patriarchal period where Jacob's sickness is mentioned (Genesis 48:1). The Old Testament

3

prophet, Isaiah, combined prophetic power with a poultice in the healing of King Heyekiah's illness (Isaiah 38:21). However, the beginning of the modern hospital can be traced clearly from early medieval times.

In fact, the etymology of the word "hospital" goes back many centuries to the Middle Ages when "Knights Hospitalers" aided crusaders and pilgrims in their travels across Europe (Risley, 1961). (The words hospice and hostel also come from the same derivation.) During this same time, tonsillectomies were being done by the "tonsorial artists" (barbers) whose blood and bandage striped insignia now give mute testimony to their former duties. Eventually, Christian charity and the practice of the healing arts merged to form our present concept of hospital. This merger solved many problems, and it also raised some profound questions about the relationship of medicine and religion which are extant today.

Physical and mental illness, while once attributed to human sin and demonic activity or both, are now viewed as proper objects of scientific inquiry. Faith healing and exorcism notwithstanding, organized religion has retreated from actual confrontation and treatment with physical and mental illness (DeHaan, N.D.). Even though medicine and psychiatry constitute the primary resources for the healing of body and mind, religion can and should contribute to man's well-being by the healing of the spirit.

Because of the holistic nature of man, it is not possible to separate effectively mental and physical functions. For even as one's perception of his body functions influences one's attitude toward himself, so also one's attitude toward himself influences the functioning of the body. Just as there is ample confirmation that emotional states are reflected in the functioning of the body (e.g., the "Fight or Flight" syndrome), it is important to consider that the functioning of the body is influenced by one's emotional and attitudinal state (e.g., psychogenic illness).

This rather nebulous "attitudinal state" involves the very essence of religion. This is because positive, constructive attitudes towards other people (trust, respect, love, etc.) as well as toward one's self (self-confidence, self-acceptance, self-esteem, etc.) are the major concerns of religion. Moreover, one of the functions of religion is to give an ethic or standard of behavior which establishes what attitudes are not only desirable but necessary for the survival of society (Collins, 1973). Ideally, it also provides the motivation and power to live by the ethic. Religion by its very nature seeks to regulate and elevate man's relationship to his fellow and himself.

It is at this point that science and religion meet. For example, induced abortion is not a complicated medical procedure, but its performance raises very complicated moral and ethical questions. More and more as scientific medicine is capable of greater and greater accomplishments (genetic engineering, organ transplants, etc.), it becomes evident that an ethic is necessary to provide a basis for making decisions of propriety and priority. It is contended, therefore, that even though their methodology does differ, religion and scientific medicine can, and indeed should, compliment each other (Martin, 1961).

The scientific method applied to the field of medicine has been highly productive. Modern science and modern medicine have gone hand in hand. Even before the advent of the germ theory of disease, empiricism was yielding a vast store of knowledge of the structure and functions of the human body. With the spectacular results in the control and abolition of many epidemic diseases, the marriage of medicine and science was solemnized.

While not discounting the obvious merits of the scientific method, the methodology employed in the study and application of religion is quite different and unique. This is because religion utilizes supernatural revelation as a means of arriving at moral and ethical truth. Supernatural revelation does not imply a nonscientific or antiscientific attitude, but it does employ a different methodology because the object of its inquiry encompasses a different dimension of human reality.

Viewed from this perspective, the difference in methodology of science and religion becomes basically an epistomological issue (O'Neill, 1961). For some, there is a diametric opposition between the scientific method as a means of discovering truth and revelation as a means of discovering truth. However, the proposition is advanced here that both methods can be immensely productive when appropriately applied. They can mutually exist, and a single individual can embrace both simultaneously. It should, therefore, be no more difficult for a person who utilizes the scientific method, such as a physician, to possess a deep and meaningful religious faith, then for a theologian to consult a physician for illness and injury.

Each method of knowing has truth as its ultimate goal (Hill, 1961). To obtain scientific truth, the scientist employs theory, observation and testing. To obtain revealed truth, the theologian must be sure that the revelation is accurately received and tested hermeneutically.

Occasionally, a scientist in selecting a theory to test may choose a theory that is contradictory to revealed truth. Further, conflicts between science and religion arise when the scientist embraces a theory which may never be able to be corroborated by observation or testing. The scientist may become emotionally involved in the defense of an untestable theory. Likewise when the theologian arrives at an interpretation of revelation which is hermeneutically untestable, conflicts arise. For he, too, may become emotionally involved in the defense of his private interpretation of revealed truth.

Until all seeming conflicts are resolved, both science and religion must approach the discovery of truth with a sense of awe that acknowledges the finitude of man and the dynamic nature of the universe. Whether one is a scholar or practitioner of science or religion, the continual realization that truth is so vast that no one person can fully appropriate all of it should help to achieve the proper perspective and balance.

As indicated, each discipline can contribute to the other. As Biblical interpretation is enhanced by the scientific methodology employed by the archaeologist, anthropologist, etc., so likewise religion can contribute to the understanding of human nature as well as provide a basis upon which value judgments may be made. Science and religion can be complementary as each pursues in complete honesty their respective searches for scientific and religious truth.

Chapter II

The Relationship of Sin and Sickness

In all kinds of calamity and adversity, the human mind seeks for rather specific answers to the question of causation. The tendency to place blame and affix responsibility for problems and difficulties seems innate in all of us. Such questions as "What did I do to deserve this?" and "Why did this have to happen to me?" are almost stock reactions to any tragedy or suffering.

A day seldom goes by for the pastoral counselor without his being asked these questions in one form or another. The particular circumstances vary, but the intensity of the inquiry never changes. It must be determined, first of all, whether the raising of these questions reflects a genuine desire for an academic or theological reply, or if the questions are simply expressions of vented frustrations. More often at the time of trauma, it is the latter. However, after the initial emotional impact of tragedy subsides, a sincere quest for answers that will make some meaning out of what has happened will often be undertaken.

At this point, the pastoral counselor must be able to interpret in an elementary way the related concepts of natural law and human will and the nature of sin. Natural law involves, among other things, the laws of probability and chances. Thus, "accidents" are probabilities that can be calculated and expressed in terms of risk. Also, various diseases have fairly stable mortality rates that are demonstrable.

When a patient contracts a certain illness, his chances of survival are known. Further, the probability one will contract a given illness or be hospitalized is based on known actuarial data. In theological interpretation, it should be noted to the patient that natural law operates indiscriminately. Saint and sinner alike are subject to its occurrence.

At the same time, human will operates independently of natural law. That is, a person can choose (in most cases) their dietary intake, amount of exercise taken, degree of exposure to noxious elements, etc. Many illnesses can be caused by the neglect of known hygienic procedures.

Sin, in its larger theological meaning, is unwholeness. Sin is ubiquitous. No human being is by nature perfectly whole and sound physically. Genetic imperfection affects all; harmful bacteria and viruses are endemic. Eventual physical death is inevitable. Everyone born will die at some time. Death is caused by sin in the final analysis. Death will come to all as a result of illness or accident, voluntarily or involuntarily. Thus, do natural law and human will combine to determine the when and how of death. Sin is the why.

God's remedy for sin is salvation, wholeness. Wholeness of man's body, mind and spirit is His ultimate purpose for man. The pastoral counselor is a representative of God and communicates to men the message of God's love and ultimate purpose for all. God promises immediate healing of man's unwhole spirit and the eventual salvation (wholeness) of his body and psyche. Complete wholeness, integration, salvation is provided, but physical and mental perfection will not be realized fully in the present life.

These concepts are necessary to the pastoral counselor's addressing the question of individual tragedy and catastrophe. However, first of all, the pastoral counselor must be sensitive to the need of a person to raise these kinds of questions. A religious patient or family member may need to be encouraged to verbalize these concepts, and he may even feel guilty expressing them to another person. Part of the pastoral counselor's role here is to assure the individual that asking "why" is not a lapse or weakness of religious faith, but a legitimate human emotion to be experienced without recrimination.

Each person needs to delve into the mystery of apparent evil, tolerated if not ordained by a loving, good God. The search for answers to the unanswerable gives the pastoral counselor a unique opportunity to help the person work through many of his feelings and theological misconceptions. The following approach and biblical exposition is included here as one of many possible avenues in the search for theological meaning one may traverse. It is not intended as a formula but as a possible model which may be built upon or partially or totally discarded.

A certain sense of guilt and responsibility when a catastrophe strikes is often projected upon us by those about us. In biblical times, three of Job's comforters tried hard to assign to his secret faults the burden of his disaster. Even in Jesus' disciples, the need to find a source to blame was evident. One classic passage which deals with this is that concerning the man born blind (Martin, 1961). In this instance, they asked the Lord, "Who sinned? This man or his parents that he was born blind." (John 9:2).

Blindness in ancient Judea was, if anything, even worse than in modern times. With no social and governmental agencies and programs to assist, the blind person was almost always an automatic beggar, dependent on the mercy and generosity of others. This particular blind man was not blinded by illness or accident, but was blind since birth. This raised in the disciples' minds a moral problem. Since, in their reasoning, blindness was a tragedy occasioned by someone's culpability, the problem of placing blame was complicated by its existence since birth. This raised the possibility of someone other than the victim himself being responsible.

Their question assumes that the blindness was a condition brought on by human sin. It was not asked if human sin was the causation factor, but rather whose sin was to blame. This linkage of sin and sickness persists in the minds of many people in time of catastrophe in the present age. Not only in the minds of primitive peoples who hear in the roar of thunder the displeasure of their gods, but also in the thinking of highly educated persons does this tendency abide.

Taking the disciples' question a step at a time will illustrate the futility of such an approach. This is not to deny that God cannot or does not discipline and chasten human beings by adversity. However, it is unproductive to imagine that each misfortune in life is hurled upon us by an angry and vengeful Creator in a direct and necessary cause and effect relationship.

I. *Blaming the Blind Man.* If indeed the blind man himself is responsible for his being born blind, there are three possibilities. The first one is that the blindness is the result of pre-natal sin. This, of course, would be difficult if not impossible to prove. It is open to question if an unborn fetus is even capable of sinning. In the birth of Jacob and Esau, it was Jacob the supplanter who grasped his elder brother's foot. This might be interpreted as a struggle *in utero* and suggest greed and avarice on the part of Jacob. Further, it is recorded that John the Baptist "leaped for joy" while his mother was six months pregnant at the greeting of her cousin Mary. Assumedly, if a wholesome emotion such as joy can be ascribed to the unborn, then perhaps it would have been possible that an unwholesome, sinful emotion could have been experienced by the man born blind.

The problem with accepting this explanation is that the man born blind would have been punished for a sinful "deed" of which he could never have had any real knowledge or memory. This kind of judgment on the part of God is so out of character of God's righteousness which is based upon fairness and equity.

A second possibility is that the man's blindness was the punishment of predestined sin. That is, God in his foreknowledge knew he would be a greater sinner if he were born sighted rather than blind. Blindness then is a judgment on sins he would have committed. Also it could be argued that the blindness was the judgment on sins he did actually commit even though blind. In either case the accusation is untenable.

Again, the very justice of God is maligned if it is suggested that He punishes sin even before it is perpetrated. This is not the same as saying that God intervenes in human life to restrain human sin. Further, to say that God punishes before sin is even committed severely limits the grace and power of God to deliver from the temptation of evil.

A third possibility is that blindness is the punishment for the man's *imputed sin;* that is, sin which is reckoned because of Adam's fall. This has a certain theological rationale in that Paul teaches that the imputation of Christ's righteousness is ignored. Further, since all men are not born blind God's justice becomes discriminatory in singling out this particular man for punishment for sin which is imputed to all.

II. *Blaming the Blind Man's Parents.* If the blame for this man's blindness cannot easily rest with him, then the disciples raise the question of his parent's culpability. There are three possibilities in which this may be thought to be the answer to their question. First, is the biblical account of David and Bathsheba's baby. The baby boy became sick after his birth and subsequently died (2 Sam. 11, 12). The child was the product of an adulterous union to be sure and the prophet, Nathan, exposed David's sin and pronounced that the judgment would be not David's death, but the death of the child.

In trying to cover his sin, David had planned the murder of Bathsheba's husband, Urijah. Inasmuch as the child born was a living offspring of David, its death expiated the Mosaic Law which dictated life for life. The child was obviously innocent of any wrongdoing and its death indeed was in judgment of the parents. Obviously, however, multitudes of children of adulterous unions are not so judged with either death or blindness. For the man born blind, the blindness is not necessarily the result of the sins of the parents, but it is much more of a possibility than its being the result of his own sins. However, it would seem somewhat arbitrary and capricious of God to so act in this case.

Further, a second possibility is intimated at least by the Mosaic Law which indicates judgment may be extended to the third and fourth generation in the case of idolatry (Exo. 20:5). In order to establish that this is the case of the man born blind, information concerning his ancestry would be necessary. Also, an assumption would have to be made that his blindness was the specific judgment intended to be administered to his forebearers.

Thirdly, the proposition that the man's blindness is a direct result of his parents' actions may be viewed from the perspective of medical consequences. It is known, for example, that the contraction of German Measles (Rubella) by a mother during the first trimester of pregnancy may cause blindness in the neonate. However, a mother's exposure to the disease would have to be deliberate and calculated with full knowledge of the probable results for this to be construed as "sin."

Thus, it seems difficult at best to ascribe the man's blindness to his parents' sin as a necessary and direct cause and effect relationship. This leaves the question basically open and unanswered. It is still not certain who is to blame if the man's blindness is seen as a punishment from God for anyone's sin.

14

Jesus' answer does not discount the possibility that the man's blindness *could* be the consequence of someone's sin. He rather shifts the focus to an entirely new dimension. He affirms that at least in this instance neither possibility is forced. Instead of being on the horns of a dilemma, our Lord opens the disciples' eyes to a perspective they had been unable to attain on their own. He says that the meaning and purpose of this particular catastrophe is to the end that the works of God might be manifest. That is, God will be glorified as a result of this apparent human tragedy. However, this does not mean that God is insensitive to the real pain that adversity brings. He is genuinely compassionate and offers to "suffer with" those who are afflicted. As a representative of God, the pastoral counselor should communicate that he sincerely regrets a patients' illness but will love and support the patient throughout the course of the illness.

How God can be glorified, especially as it applies to the broader area of human misfortune, can be explored in three directions. First of all, as it happened to the man born blind, a miracle of healing can take place. God is glorified and His work is evident when a miraculous deliverance from any human suffering takes place. God is not bound to heal by the skill and wisddom of his creatures alone. If it is His will and pleasure, He will heal the human situation immediately— that is, with no mediating agency. God will not be limited or restricted in the demonstration of His love and power.

Secondly, a miracle takes place when human tragedy and misfortune elicits love and compassion in the hearts of those not so afflicted. It is an evident work of God that moves in the hearts of His creatures to reach out and minister to the needs of others. Going counter to the basic selfish instincts in man, human compassion is a divine accomplishment. It is possible that one intended by-product of human suffering is the sympathy and empathy of other human beings.

15

Whenever help is rendered to another (even the giving of a cup of cold water) motivated by the love of Christ, God is glorified.

A third miracle that may result from the plight of human suffering is the supply of sufficient grace. God is glorified when endurance equal to the evil is given. An adequate measure of grace is a work of God and comes directly from Him. Paul experienced this in relation to his own suffering (2 Cor. 12). Church history is replete with examples of unbelievable human suffering encountered and triumphed over by the grace of God. Perhaps another clue to the mystery of human suffering is that it gives occasion to experience the sufficiency of God in situations that cannot be changed or manipulated by any human being.

While there has to be a certain tentativeness about any definite conclusions in any specific circumstances, it seems that the answer of our Lord might apply to most instances of human misery today. It is not so much a question of determining whose sin is causing the particular misfortune, but rather a question of determining which of these or other ways God will be glorified. Shifting the focus away from ourselves and others is in itself the beginning of the miracle God has in store. Perhaps instead of asking "Why me?" a more constructive and productive question might be "What, Lord?"

Ideally, the pastoral counselor can assist the patient and/or his family move from an unproductive search for guilt and blame, and enable them to move freely in a more constructive direction. This task is often difficult, but the benefits accrued are well worth the investment of the pastoral counselor's time and energy. More than anyone else, he stands in a position of rendering a great service which will nullify or minimize an undesirable emotional reaction to illness, suffering and loss.

16

Often, however, the pastoral counselor is limited in pursuing the concept of adversity from this perspective because of the patient's weak or lack of faith. In these circumstances, the pastoral counselor can develop the theme that catastrophe is distributed arbitrarily by laws of chance and that the possibility of misfortune is not discriminatory. Somehow the realization that trouble comes to all in various forms and at various times may help the individual work through some of the resentment and hostility which occurs in time of tragedy. To feel that one's own problems are unique is overwhelming indeed, and to realize that others have problems as bad or worse is often some degree of consolation.

Also, the pastoral counselor must bear in mind the powerful adverse effect that conscious and deliberate sin has on physical health. Reference was made in the preceding chapter to psychogenic illness. Sin, as an unwholesome state of mind, can be responsible for this kind of sickness. The role of the pastoral counselor in these instances is to emphasize the concept of forgiveness (Martin, 1961). In helping a person work through feelings of guilt, the stage is set for a physical healing as well as a spiritual cleansing.

In any event, the pastoral counselor can be instrumental in comforting the believer, and agnostic alike, varying his approach to meet the patient and/or the patient's family wherever they are spiritually. Sensitivity to this dimension will greatly enhance the usefulness of the pastoral counselor.

Chapter III

Theological Aspects of Suffering

A wild deer darted out in front of a young woman's car and caused the car to swerve into the on-coming traffic. As a result of the terrible collision, the young mother's car was demolished, and she was badly hurt. The damage to her legs was such that it was necessary to surgically remove one of her limbs. In time of such a personal catastrophe and calamity, there is a natural inclination to question the goodness of God.

The very presence of evil in a world created by a loving omnipotent God appears to be an unresolvable dilemma. If God is loving, why is there any suffering at all? If God is all-powerful, why does He permit evil to exist and continue? These questions, in a variety of forms, confront the pastoral counselor daily.

Also, the theological implications of human suffering are interwoven with the psychological needs of the patient. For some patients, suffering is man's lot and to be expected and borne as well as possible. The pastoral counselor will even come in contact with the small minority of patients who demonstrate religious masochism. These patients seem to need to suffer because of inner guilt feelings that are resolved by their pain. They differ radically from patients who do not enjoy suffering, but do enjoy the extra attention that physical illness produces from their relatives, friends and hospital personnel. The true masochist is motivated by the need to hurt, the other is motivated by the need for succorance. Although both types of patients seem almost to relish physical distress, their respective motivations are quite different.

The pastoral counselor will need to be able to distinguish between these two types of sufferers. For the one who experiences a religious catharsis in suffering, the pastoral counselor may need to refer such for in-depth psychotherapy; for the other a little extra tender, loving care may be all that is needed. Generally, the patient himself will drop obvious clues as to his emotional response to his suffering.

For example, the pastoral counselor might make the open-ended observation, "You seem to be very uncomfortable today." The masochist may well reply, "Yes, but Christ had to suffer more." or "We all have to have our share of suffering here on earth." On the other hand, the response might be, "Yes, but it even hurt worse yesterday." The one reacts in religious or philosophic terms and the other in more pragmatic and quantitative measures. The pastoral counselor needs to be sensitive to the differing needs of the patient who suffers. Further, the amount of pain medication requested may indicate the underlying motivation.

Yet another type of sufferer is the patient whose threshold for pain is exceedingly low. His reaction to pain is real to him, but medically does not seem justified. Assuming the patient is not addicted to narcotics already, this patient may be very anxious. These feelings of anxiety might be unrelated to the illness, *per se*, but manifest themselves in accentuated pain sensitivity. The pastoral counselor can be very helpful at this point in giving genuine assurances and encouraging the patient to talk about whatever is bothering him.

In any event, there seems to emerge three inter-related questions which are asked in various forms by those who are faced with trauma and tragedy. These are: (1) Why didn't God prevent it? (2) Why Doesn't God stop it? and (3) Why doesn't God do something? Although one can never fully understand the totality of God's plan, one can gain increasing insight into the questions which are occasioned by loss and suffering. For each of these questions raised, there is a biblical parallel which helps to answer them. These questions and Scripture portions will be discussed in the order presented above.

I. WHY DIDN'T GOD PREVENT IT?

The first question encompasses the whole range of human experience which we designate as "accidents." It was raised very eloquently by both sisters of Lazarus when their brother died. Each sister points out to Jesus, "Lord, if you had been here, my brother would not have died." (John 11:21, 32). Their statements can be interpreted and expressed in question form: "Lord, why didn't you prevent this dire event from occurring?"

The pivot of their statements is the "if." All tragic occurrences could have been avoided "if . . . " Whether the accident involves non-human objects such as cars as in the instance related above or whether the tragedy centers on disease germs or body malfunction as in the case of Lazarus, the damage done is often irreversible and immense.

Why did Jesus tarry beyond the Jordan when He was needed in Bethany to heal the illness of Lazarus? *If* Jesus would have arrived in time, He could have laid his hands on Lazarus and prayed for him and healed him. In the case of the mother's accident, why did a deer happen to run in front of the young woman's car at precisely a time and place to cause the collision? If the animal had not hit the car or if no traffic had been coming in the other lane, the accident would not have happened. Was God off duty? Did He not care? Could God not prevent all the evil that exists in the universe and especially that which makes for the tragedies of human life?

The obvious answer to these questions is not particularly satisfying. Yes, God could conceivably prevent the ill that befalls each of his children. The significant aspect is that He does not. Therefore, we are driven by faith to conclude

21

that God permits the storms and stresses that converge upon us for our best good.

The problem with this is that our definition of "good" is conditioned more by our finitude than by our faith. The basic materialism and selfishness of human nature defines good in terms of what we want and not in terms of what is for our ultimate best interest. Since God's thoughts and ways are infinite, we take it that our tragedy, grief and sorrow have a redeeming quality that we often cannot comprehend. It is only by faith that we accept that which we cannot understand. Faith accepts the wisdom of God sight unseen.

The answer to the question of why God does not prevent that which causes us pain and hurt is simply that somehow, in some way, it benefits us. More often than not we can see the redemptive purpose of suffering in the lives of others before we can see it in relation to our own. It takes all the faith we can muster in time of apparent defeat and disaster to believe that any good can emerge from such an experience.

Death is the ultimate human loss. It often shatters our brittle faith and like Mary and Martha we question the intentions of the Master. If faith does not triumph, the alternative is a debilitating bitterness.

In counseling with those who have lost someone dear, the pastoral counselor should not pretend to know how their particular loss fits into a plan of Divine reason and purpose. Know only that on this side of Heaven, it hurts and a ministry of comfort is needed. A great part of comfort consists in the reaffirmation of God's wisdom and the reassurance of His all-encompassing love.

II. WHY DOESN'T GOD STOP IT?

The second question is related to the first and differs only in its application. In the classic case the evil is now more chronic than acute. When the pastoral counselor visits terminally ill patients the question they often ask is, "Why can't I die?" "Why must I linger?" "Why doesn't God stop my suffering?"

One elderly lady lay for many months in the hospital with very few visitors to see her. In early visits, the pastoral counselor would ask if there was anything he could do for her or help her in any way. She always replied, "No." But after about a month, she asked him to pray for her. She had no church or religious preference. Thereafter, if he failed to suggest prayer, she would remind him. Over the many weeks the pastoral counselor called upon her, there was detected a spiritual growth and understanding in the questions she asked and the conversations engaged in. God was dealing with her in a definite way, preparing her for an eternal relationship with Him. Certainly not every instance of terminal illness accomplishes this purpose, but at least in this one case God was working a miracle of grace in her heart. Often, however, the pastoral counselor has no indication of what God's purpose may be in any given instance.

The Apostle Paul also asked by implication, "Why doesn't God take away my misery?" Paul refers to his "thorn in the flesh" from which he asked deliverance. (II Corinthians 12:7-10) In fact, he prayed three times asking for the removal of this physical impairment, but God's answer was "no." His thorn in the flesh was perhaps a reference to Paul's eye trouble. Some Biblical scholars believe that Paul's use of others in copying his letters indicates a visual handicap of some sort.

Whatever the physical faculty or ability involved, it affected Paul so that it became a matter of his earnest prayer for relief. So strongly he sought deliverance that he prayed three times. Note that the answer to this prayer for healing was not contingent upon the amount or quality of Paul's faith, but was based upon the will and purpose of God for him. Not all illness befalls us because of lack of faith, nor is deliverance automatic in the presence of faith. God's greater glory con-

23

sisted in Paul's bearing up under his affliction rather than in his relief from the affliction.

Our society's frenetic way of life has made "instant relief" a nationally advertised good. In God's economy, however, His purpose may well be realized in one's relying more fully upon His grace. The pastoral counselor may find that if, in the face of repeated prayers for release and deliverance, God permits continual suffering, there is purpose. God is not capricious or sadistic; He is touched by His children's sicknesses and knows their infirmities. It becomes necessary to look beyond the temporal into the eternal in order to accept human suffering as it is. Lack of comprehension and understanding makes it difficult to accept the proposition that "all things work together for good." (Romans 8:28)

As mentioned above, the second question is an extension of the first and the answer reached is basically the same. The inability to view life as God does, prevents one from seeing life in its true perspective. Basic humanity limits the concept of suffering to a very narrow dimension and finds it extremely difficult to see beyond the here and now. If faith does not triumph, the alternative is hopelessness and despair. The proof of God's love for man may not necessarily consist of His not experiencing pain and suffering, but in experiencing His love for man in that suffering.

III. WHY DOESN'T GOD DO SOMETHING?

This third question also is an extension of the same problem of evil. However, the focus is on the supposed inactivity of God to initiate a set of circumstances which is seemingly desirable. A pastoral counselor was talking with a woman who was visiting a relative at the hospital. In the discussion, she revealed that she and her husband had no children, but desperately wanted a family. They lived on a farm and were well fixed financially; they were a devout Christian couple. They had prayed continually asking God to permit them to have a child of their own. She mentioned

24

cases of children who were born unwanted and were often neglected and abused, and she asked why God did not answer their prayer.

There are many examples in the Scriptures of God not responding to our wishes. One is contained in the Book of Jonah. Jonah finally reached Nineveh and declared his message of God's judgment. When the city repented of its evil and God withheld His punishment, Jonah was displeased and angry. He assumed a position of watch to see if the city would be overthrown as he had prophesied. God's decision to avert punishment in the light of their repentance was infuriating to Jonah. His complaint might be paraphrased, "Why doesn't God send the judgment He told me to proclaim?"

The position of Jonah was obviously untenable, and God illustrated this by the lesson of the gourd. The ongoing purpose of God, God's consistency within Himself, God's triumphant grace over sin were revealed in spite of Jonah's petulance. Often patients' find themselves in Jonah's role. They are sure that their position is correct and theologically defensible, and thus assail God with the logic of their prayer. When God fails to do what they think best, they ask, "Why doesn't God do something?" Whether it is the conception of a child or the destruction of a city, it is felt that God is remiss and unmindful of their good when He does not immediately instigate the program they want.

Many seemingly desirable events do not come to pass. Even the pastoral counselor is prone to think that God has forsaken His cause and His people. From a purely earthly vantage point, one indulges in a sense of defeat and frustration, forgetting that God's wisdom far supercedes man's own. The only alternative to this frustration is faith - believing that God's timing is never errant, even though all seems lost. This faith is demonstrated by Martha's statement when it seems Jesus had waited too long to help. She said, ". . . I

25

know that *even now* whatever You ask of God, He will grant you." (John 11:22)

The essence of faith is seeing what is not visible, believing what is not possible. Always it is to the greater glory of God when He does not do what we want Him to do, when we want it. It is difficult for a patient to accept this proposition when his faith is tried in the furnace of affliction and suffering. The pastoral counselor needs to point out that when God fails to perform according to man's desire and expectation, it is always for his ultimate good and God's greater glory.

The patient and his family need to be reminded of the exclamation of the Apostle Paul" "O the depth of the wealth, the wisdom and the knowledge of God! How inscrutable are His judgments and how untraceable His footsteps! . . . For from Him, and through Him and to Him are all things. To Him by glory forever! Amen." (Romans 11:33, 36) The extent that the pastoral counselor can communicate this trust is the extent to which he can alleviate some of the spiritual anguish that usually accompanies physical suffering.

Chapter IV

Religious Needs and Creeds of the Patient

The psycho-social concept of the "whole man" is reflected in the current concept of "total patient care." Whereas ancient philosophers attempted to dissect man into segments labeled body, soul and spirit, the task of the modern physician, psychologist and theologian is to make man whole again. In spite of current efforts there persists a pragmatic fragmentation of the hospital patient. Fortunately, the trend is toward greater mutual respect and cooperation among the medical, paramedical and auxiliary staff in the hospital. The recognition of the basic unity of man will result in better patient care.

Proceeding on the proposition that it is basically impossible to divide the hospital patient into parts, it is readily apparent that anything that profoundly affects a man affects his whole being. That is, when physical trauma is present, it follows that all of the patient is subjected to stress and tension. Further, the degree of physical trauma is reflected proportionately throughout the entire individual. Thus the greater the stress placed on the body, the greater the likelihood of the disintegration of the whole person. The purpose of this discussion is to focus on the corollary effects of "unwholeness" or illness which can be described as religious or spiritual. However, to speak of religious needs does not imply a real division of man, but is merely a semantic convenience.

A partial listing of the religious needs of a patient might include: the need to believe in the infinite—that which is greater than one's self, the need to affiliate and associate with those who hold similar beliefs, the need to explain phenomena beyond our present knowledge, and to have a set of standards by which we can establish an ethic—a right way of life.

The way by which one satisfies these seemingly universal needs makes a profound difference in the attitude one has toward himself and his environment. A person entering the hospital does not divest himself of his religious attitudes and values. Indeed, these may well be intensified. An awareness of this fact increases the pastoral counselor's ability to relate the "whole man." Needless to say, he will be requested to counsel with many patients who seek to satisfy their religious needs by radically different processes than his own. Tolerance for and acceptance of the variety of religious experiences employed by others without feeling threatened is as necessary as accepting the patient's race, politics or personality.

While the pastoral counselor is well aware of the interrelationship between physical, psychological and spiritual needs, he should also be cognizant of the distinctive religious practices of the patients he counsels. Following this principle will result in better rapport, while ignoring it can produce anxiety and anger on the part of the patient. Briefly, some of these distinctive needs will be discussed next.

(1) *Roman Catholic Patients.* For the pastoral counselor there are several points that need to be appreciated in relation to the Catholic patient. The Catholic Church teaches the necessity of infant baptism because of original sin. This being the case, the pastoral counselor visiting in the obstetri-

cal ward should be very careful to alert a priest if an infant is critical so that baptism can be administered immediately. In fact, if the arrival of the priest is delayed for any reason he may wish the pastoral counselor to baptize the baby himself. Water can be contained in a cup and sprinkled on the baby's head, and the simple baptismal formula employed: "(Name of child), I baptize you in the Name of the Father, Son and Holy Spirit. Amen." If this is performed in case of an emergency, the priest should be advised of this for purposes of keeping parish records since the sacrament of baptism is not repeatable.

Similarly, the priest should be notified if other patients of any age show low vital signs. This is to allow for the Sacrament of Anointing the Sick which is performed on behalf of the patient. Even when the patient is not responding or comatose, the priest should be summoned. If the patient should expire before the priest can arrive, the priest will still administer the sacrament inasmuch as there is not universal agreement as to the exact moment of death.

Another consideration of the spiritual needs of the Catholic patient is the Confessional. During this Sacrament, it is greatly appreciated if there is as little interruption as possible on the part of the hospital staff. Yet another Sacrament of importance to the Roman Catholic patient is Communion which is administered individually in the hospital. Generally speaking, arrangements for this are taken care of by the priest, and it is usually administered in the early morning.

(2) *Protestant Patients.* It is more difficult to delineate the religious needs of the Protestant patient because of the variety of religious expression employed. Baptism would be a case in point. Basically, there are two Protestant views about baptism. One group of churches subscribes to the practice of pedo-baptism or infant baptism. These churches include the Methodist, Presbyterian, Lutheran, Episcopal,

the United Church of Christ, and others. On the other hand, the Baptist, Christian and Seventh Day Adventist churches are firm in their belief in the efficacy of adult baptism only. Adult is interpreted as the "age of accountability" and may chronologically occur during the pre-teen years, and baptism is understood to refer to complete immersion only. Therefore, if the baby of a Baptist mother, for example, is critical, her pastor would want to be contacted, but his purpose in coming would not be to baptize the infant. Whereas the Roman Catholic patient would be greatly comforted in the knowledge that her baby had been baptized if critical, the Baptist mother would be upset and offended.

The Quakers, however, do not believe in ritual baptism at any age, by any mode, but affirm an "inner baptism." Although their theological position is similar to that of our Protestants, they are distinctive in their disdain for any rites or ceremonies. This means that the Quaker mother would not want her neonate baptized. Likewise, the Quakers would not want any special religious rites for the critically ill of any age. Generally, the Quakers have no clergy, but a clerk of the meeting may be informed of a critical illness; however, he would come only as one of the members of the group—not on behalf of the meeting.

For the Quaker, death is but the natural end of life; it is to be accepted simply and practically. They feel that the funeral should likewise be as simple as possible. Therefore, the Quaker family may not want a local funeral director called, but they will likely have made independent arrangements themselves.

Most Protestant groups have no religious dietary restrictions. However, Seventh Day Adventists recommend (but do not demand) that their members adhere to a vegetarian diet. While a matter of individual conscience, most Adventists follow what they call an "ovo-lacto" diet which includes adequate protein intake. If meat is eaten, only those which are "clean" (beef, chicken, most fish) are used. Pork and shellfish are avoided. No drinks containing caffeine, such as coffee, tea and cola, are recommended, but Adventists will drink cereal-derived products such as Postum. Latter Day Saints (Mormons) drink neither coffee or tea also.

Another aspect of patient care about which the pastoral counselor should be alert is the position of the Jehovah's Witnesses on blood transfusions. This Protestant sect teaches that blood transfusions under any circumstances are sinful and forbidden for its members (Blood, Medicine and the Law of God, 1961). The group is not opposed to I.V. feeding of dextrose, glucose, etc., but receiving blood in any form by any method is strongly denounced. The devout Jehovah's Witness may carry a card on their person indicating this prohibition and containing a list of the fluids that may be used in place of blood in case of emergency and the patient is not conscious.

Currently, in the wake of the charismatic movement, there is increased interest among many Protestant denominations in "faith healing." This belief in its most simplistic form is that if the individual has enough faith, then a miraculous healing will follow. This healing may occur with or without the mediacy of a minister. This attitude may complicate patient care because in extreme instances, a hospitalized patient of this persuasion may actually refuse or resist therapeutic measures prescribed by the physician. Generally, religious groups that call themselves "apostolic" or "pentecostal" are more apt to display this tendency (Martin, 1961). In this case, the pastoral counselor must be sure to put the best interest of the patient first firmly, yet lovingly.

Related to the attitude that physical medicine is of use only to those whose faith is weak is the position of the Christian Scientist. The Mother Church specifically teaches against mixing healing methods (Eddy, 1895). This means that faithful adherents will not seek a "matter physician"

31

while a Christian Science Practitioner, a "metaphysician," is treating them. Generally, the ardent student Christian Scientist will not come to the hospital at all, since many practitioners will not work in a hospital. Although medicine, drugs and surgery are considered unnecessary, a nurse who administers drugs to a Christian Scientist who has had an accident and is not conscious will suffer no recrimination.

The Christian Scientist believes that disease is not real and that human means as aids to healing should be avoided. The pastoral counselor may come into contact with a patient whose convictions are not strong and who seeks conventional medical assistance. Having some acquaintance with the religious background of this type of patient may help the pastoral counselor understand the inner conflicts and anxieties he may be experiencing.

(3) *Jewish Patients.* The degree to which the Jewish religious faith affects the patient's hospitalization will probably be the degree of tradition he embraces. The Reform Jew will not be as concerned as either the Orthodox or Conservative about dietary restrictions, observance of the Sabbath, and other customs.

The Jewish faith is centered in the home as well as in the synagogue, so that if a Jewish patient is in the hospital on the high holy days he may be despondent and want to be at home. Especially the feasts of Passover, Tabernacles and Weeks are traditionally celebrated in the home.

To all Jews, the rite of circumcision is of great significance. This ritual is observed on the eighth day of the infant's life, and it denotes the covenant between God and the newborn male child. Circumcision is performed by the Rabbi himself or one specially designated from the congregation, the *Mohel*. In some cases, the physician may do it with a Rabbi present. The rite usually takes place in the morning or afternoon and is followed by a celebration and a light meal. A nurse may be requested to sterilize the instruments which the Rabbi brings with him (a ceremonial knife and a shield), but the ceremony itself is private. Hospital accommodations permitting, the circumcision is done in a room adjoining the mother's. With the length of maternity stay being shortened, the rite of circumcision is more often done in the outpatient unit or in the home.

Another important facet of pastoral care of the Jewish patient is the necessity of calling the Rabbi if the patient's condition is critical. Generally, the family of the patient will do this if circumstances permit. However, if the family cannot be reached, the pastoral counselor should definitely call the Rabbi on his own, so that the Jewish patient would not be alone when he expires (Bollinger, 1969).

The Jewish belief about amputation and autopsy are of significance to the Orthodox. The amputated limb, for example, is often accorded burial rather than incineration at the hospital. Unless special circumstances prevail, the Orthodox tradition forbids an autopsy to be performed. Exceptions to this would include the mandate of the state, or if death was not attributed to natural causes. On the other hand, the liberal Jewish tradition encourages both autopsy and amputation when advised by the physician. Each individual Jewish family should be encouraged to seek the advice of their Rabbi when these controversial and emotional decisions need to be made.

Reference has already been made to the special or kosher diet of the traditional Jew. Generally, the prohibition on proscribed foods includes meat that has not been ritually prepared. Even certain combinations of kosher foods, such as the simultaneous serving of meat and milk products, is forbidden. The hospital dietitian is usually aware of these dietary considerations, but the pastoral counselor should also have a general concept of these beliefs.

(4) *Oriental Patients*. Often in large urban areas, the pastoral counselor will encounter patients who are adherents of Oriental religions. Many of these religions will also be encountered by chaplains serving with the military. There are at least two general characteristics of Oriental religions that are of special concern to the pastoral counselor. One is their basic fatalism, as in Islam; the other is their concept of death and reincarnation, as in Buddhism.

Fatalism is simply the belief that what will be is determined by fate and cannot be altered or avoided. Therefore, if a person becomes ill he was meant to be ill and accepts it on that basis. Illness also may be conceived as punishment resulting from past actions in a previous life. Thus there may be no real desire to recover or to seek proper medical attention.

Reincarnation is the belief that after death life continues in another form. That is, a person may be reborn as an animal in his next life. Hence, the strong belief in the sanctity of all living things (such as cattle in India). Until a soul becomes pure and achieves nothingness (*Nirvana*), he may be reincarnated many times. Death is not viewed with the struggle and finality of our Western culture. The pastoral counselor may find these attitudes quite foreign to his own and difficult to deal with.

(5) *American Indian Patients*. Though the greatest geographical concentration of Indian reservations is in the Southwest, pastoral counselors encounter Indian patients in every section of the country. Virtually hundreds of tribes, each of which have their own language and culture, have been distinguished. The specific religious beliefs of each of the various tribes also differ tremendously. However, a common strand running through each is a basic animism, or spirit worship. This belief, expressed in a large variety of ways, invests ordinary objects and phenomena with life and often with supernatural power.

34

In view of the Indian's religious association with the work of nature, it is understandable that when he is taken from the reservation and his family, a considerable degree of loneliness and apprehension overtakes him. Compounding this is the language barrier which may make it difficult for the pastoral counselor to communicate, and often it is necessary to consult an interpreter. If the hospital is located in an area where several tribes are served, it is to the pastoral counselor's advantage to compile a list of interpreters of the various languages and dialects who are willing to come to the hospital and assist in communicating with the patient.

These, then, are some of the religious distinctives and needs which the pastoral counselor may encounter in his hospital visiting. For the pastoral counselor to have an appreciation of patients' special religious needs will enable him to counsel more effectively. A lack of appreciation and attention to these needs may cause needless offense to those whom he may be called upon to serve.

Chapter V

Spiritual Therapy

The interaction between the pastoral counselor and the hospital patient must be, if nothing else, therapeutic. If his visit in any way interferes with the best good and well-being of the patient, the pastoral counselor has been remiss. This is not to say that there will never be any personality conflicts or fundamental and unresolvable theological differences in the interpersonal exchange between patient and pastoral counselor. It does mean that the deliberate goal of their contact is the welfare of the patient.

The pastoral counselor, often by virtue of his ministerial office, is in a position to do a great deal of good in the hospital setting. By the same token, irreparable damage can be done. The purpose of this chapter is to examine the tools and skills needed by the pastoral counselor in increasing his effectiveness and nullifying any negative aspects of his ministry. In order to do this, three facets of what might be called "spiritual therapy" will be explored: (1) The unique character of pastoral counseling, (2) the appropriate use of prayer and Scripture reading, and (3) practical suggestions and guidelines.

The unique character of pastoral counseling. Many hospitals today have a psychiatrist on call, a resident psychologist, a social worker skilled in counseling. This being the case, the question can legitimately be raised as to the need and the contribution of the pastoral counselor. What does he bring to the counseling situation that cannot be brought by the professionals previously mentioned? The answer lies in the

37

unique character of pastoral counseling. Pastoral counseling ideally brings a plus that is often lacking in the approach of other disciplines.

In addition to a scholarly understanding of counseling psychology, the pastoral counselor has an appreciation of the human being from a religious perspective (Clinebell, 1965). This means that a view of man is held which may provide additional and differing data from that held from a purely psychological approach. Thus, the pastoral counselor will accept information from other than a rigid, experimental frame of reference. Many of these beliefs about the nature of man and the universe will profoundly influence the counseling relationship between counselor and patient.

Some of these tenets may be identified as follows: (1) That intercessory prayer is efficacious, (2) That God can heal apart from medical mediacy, (3) That Scripture and Sacrament are beneficial to emotional and physical well-being, (4) That God can enable a human being to change radically and permanently (as opposed to psychological determinism), (5) That all human beings are inherently of worth and value, (6) That human sin is an absolute reality that mitigates against man's best good, (7) That there is life after death; physical death is not an ultimate loss. These beliefs and the implicit value system they form make the pastoral counselor distinct from other helping professionals. This, of course, is not to say that a clinical psychologist or a physician may not share these same beliefs personally, but these beliefs do form the basic structure of pastoral counseling and distinguish it from other types of counseling which are devoid of these beliefs. The pastoral counselor brings to the counseling situation an additional dimension—the spiritual. He does not reject the findings of the behavioral sciences, but he does accept insights into the nature of man and physical healing from another modality as well.

This additional insight does not imply a judgmental or superior attitude on the part of the pastoral counselor. Indeed, as noted above, part of his belief includes a universal acceptance of all persons since all are intrinsically valuable. He does not see his role as a condemnatory one, but one of giving unsolicited support and active acceptance.

At the same time, the pastoral counselor believes that no one is beyond help since God is able to effect constructive change in the values and life style of all persons. The pastoral counselor, however, must be extremely aware of the possibility of manipulation by the patient. This is necessary because his religious beliefs and accepting attitude may be perceived, initially at least, as weakness and vulnerability by the counselee. The pastoral counselor must be very careful not to be used as the patient's means of striking out against his medical regimen or against the patient's family. Certainly, the pastoral counselor can and should be the patient's advocate, but he should be wary of becoming the patient's dupe.

The belief in the reality of human sin may seem to be contradictory to a belief in the worth and value of the individual and the mutability of human nature. However, a belief in the sinfulness of all persons does not confer upon the pastoral counselor a judgmental stance, as noted above. Similarly, universal human sinfulness is seen as a demonstration of the need for human beings to change and does not imply a determinism or fatalism that despairs of helping deeply troubled persons.

The appropriate use of Scripture and prayer. In his hospital ministry, the pastoral counselor should not adopt an overbearing or "pushy" role. At the same time, he should not be reluctant to employ Scripture reading and prayer as aids to the healing process. As one who sincerely believes in the efficacy of prayer for others, the pastoral counselor should be quick to pray audibly in the presence of the patient (Sanford, 1966). In a pluralistic society, he will encounter those who would not wish this to be done. Intercessory prayer for these patients can be made by the pastoral counselor at another time.

The purpose of praying in the patient's presence is not only to enlist Divine aid in healing, but also to give that patient a sense of the love and power of God and the assurance of the pastoral counselor's genuine concern for his recovery. These prayers should be brief, to the point, and mention the patient names and any aspects of the illness and treatment that are appropriate and in good taste.

The following eight prayers are illustrative of concepts that might be appropriate for various hospital patients. For most Protestant patients, a spontaneous, personal prayer is preferable to a formal, written prayer. These particular prayers have been employed as hand-outs for over six years in medical hospitals served by this writer, and have been composed by him.

Prayer For Today

Dear Father, I have learned one thing since I have been ill—to be thankful. I have not been as thankful for good health before as I am now.

I have not realized before that people—my friends, relatives and others—really do care.

Thank You for this realization. Thank You for the ministers and others from the churches who have come in Your Name to visit me while I have been ill.

Help me to be more compassionate for the sufferings of others. Thank You for suffering in my place.

May I not forget to be thankful for life and the degree of health and wholeness You have given me today. Amen. (Fig. 1-a)

Prayer For Today

Gracious God, I am nervous and upset. My soul is disquieted within me—for I am afraid. I am afraid of the unknown. I do not know how seriously ill I may or may not be. The uncertainty of my condition is making me feel uneasy.

I know, O lord, that You do love me and that whatever befalls me, You are at my side. Make me secure in the knowledge of Your love.

Take away the doubts and fears that plague me. Free me from the gloom that settles round about me.

Grant me the calm and serenity of mind and spirit that comes from casting all my care upon You, knowing that You care for me. Amen. (Fig. 1-b)

Prayer For Today

O God, I feel ashamed of myself. I am not as ill as others about me, yet I complain and feel sorry for myself.

I not only make myself miserable by indulging in self-pity—I also make those near me uncomfortable, too.

Forgive me for my selfishness and self-centeredness. Guide my path into new avenues of service and concern for others.

Help me, O Lord, to realize that as I give of myself to others, I am really giving myself to You.

Throughout my hospital stay grant me a concern for the feelings of others as well as for myself. Amen. (Fig. 1-c)

Prayer For Today

Lord, help me to understand more fully Your purpose for my life. I have had time to think about my life, my values, the direction I am going.

Give me the grace to accept what I cannot change, and the ability to change what can be changed.

Grant me new purpose in living—help me to see Your hand in all of life, to hear Your voice above the noise of living, and to feel Your presence continually.

May this spiritual awareness follow me after I leave the hospital. Enable me, O God, to remember the lessons I have learned. Amen. (Fig. 1-d)

Prayer For Today

O Lord, I am anxious and upset. I need a special measure of Your grace to keep calm and composed.

I am in a strange place and away from family and familiar faces. I am facing surgery and I am afraid.

Thank You, Lord, for giving my doctor wisdom and knowledge as he operates.

May all be done according to Your will and plan for my life.

Help me to draw on Your strength in this time of worry and apprehension. Amen. (Fig. 1-e)

Prayer For Today

Dear God, I hurt and am in pain. Sometimes my mind is confused and I do not remember all that has happened.

I ask You to ease the pain and discomfort I am feeling and help my body to heal. Help me to respond to the care and treatment I am getting.

Thank You, God, for the nurses and those who are taking care of me when I cannot take care of myself.

In my weakness help me to rely more completely in Your strength. Help me to find the peace that passes understanding through trusting in Your grace. Amen. (Fig. 1-f)

Prayer For Today

O Lord, I feel let down and discouraged. I know I should not be, but I am. I'm not in severe pain, but I'm still uncomfortable.

I am still weak and unable to do what I would like to do for myself. Help me to realize that healing takes time.

Grant me encouragement in spirit as well as strength for my body. Thank You, God, for life itself and the measure of health and soundness You have given me.

Give me the ability to accept help graciously from others. Amen. (Fig. 1-g)

Prayer For Today

Lord, I am tired of being ill. It seems so long ago that I could go and come as I pleased; it seems like a long time since I really felt good.

Yet I know I am still not ready to return home. I miss my home and loved ones; I miss all my familiar surroundings.

They take such good care of me here, but I still want to be home. Speed the healing process, O God, and give me the grace to pass the time as constructively as possible.

I have a lot of time to think—Let me think often about You. Amen. (Fig. 1-h)

Also, the use of Scripture as a means of spiritual support cannot be over-emphasized. The verbal expression of God's love and power is a very powerful therapeutic agent. Assurances that God is able and willing to heal can be extremely valuable in maximizing the patient's own spiritual potential. As with prayer, the Scripture should be selective and appropriate. The modern translations are easier to read orally and silently. A list of selected Bible passages follows with the theme or emphasis supplied by the American Bible Society. These are not arranged in any particular order or sequence.

I. *Old Testament Scripture*

Psalm 96	God the Supreme King
Psalm 46	God Is With Us
Psalm 23	The Lord Our Shepherd
Psalm 8	When I Look at Thy Heavens
Psalm 16	Preserve Me, O God
Psalm 19	The Firmament Proclaims His Handiwork
Psalm 24	The Earth Is the Lord's
Psalm 33:8-22	The Lord Looks Down from Heaven
Psalm 84	How Lovely Is Thy Dwelling Place
Psalm 91	My God, In Whom I Trust
Psalm 103:1-18	Like a Flower of the Field
Psalm 107:1-16	In Desert Wastes
Psalm 119:1-18	Blessed Are Those
Psalm 119:97-112	A Light to My Path
Psalm 121	I Lift Up My Eyes
Psalm 146	Praise the Lord

II. *New Testament Scripture*

Matthew 5:1-16	Sermon on the Mount
Matthew 6:5-15	Teaching About Prayer
Philippians 1:3-11	Paul's Prayer for His Readers
1 Corinthians 13	Love

These are just a few of the Scripture portions of the pastoral counselor may utilize to support the hospitalized patient. The Psalms seem specially adaptable for this purpose.

The pastoral counselor may also be a person for those long term patients who might desire some type of Bible study. A small collection of study booklets would be sufficient for most patients' needs. (The Gideons International supply most hospitals with copies of the Bible or New Testament with the Psalms.)

Some practical suggestions. One of the more important things the pastoral counselor needs to keep uppermost in his mind is the purpose of his visit. A common temptation is to forget that the contact with the patient is designed to meet the patient where he is spiritually and to seek to inspire and uplift him from that point. The visit should not be an "ego trip" for the pastoral counselor, and he should not use the patient for his own ego satisfaction. To this end, the pastoral counselor must continually examine his motives. The tendency for many is to visit those patients who make one feel needed more often and longer than those who do not. Real giving of one's self is to give with no thought of return. Assuredly, this is more difficult, demanding and exhausting. It is also the most needed.

To enhance the effectiveness of the pastoral counselor's hospital visitation, the following twelve points and the rationale behind them are offered. These are the product of this writer's hospital experience.

1. *KNOCK before entering a patient's room*—even if the door is partially or completely open, it is a signal that you respect the patient's right to privacy. Also, an open door may mean that the last person in the room forgot to close it, and the patient was not able to get up and close it. A closed door may mean that a humidifier is in use or that the patient is being bathed or examined by the physician. A good policy is to check with a floor nurse if the door is closed.

2. *Walk and talk softly*—when a patient is not feeling well (which is why he is hospitalized) noises are often accentuated and annoying. It is a small courtesy also to other patients besides the one you are visiting to be as quiet as possible.

3. *Shake hands only at the patient's request*—a handshake is an excellent greeting under normal circumstances, but hospitalization is not a normal circumstance. The patient may have, or recently had, an IV in his arm and to reach for his hand and give it a rigorous shake could be very painful. If the patient has had a recent injection in his arm, a handshake would not be welcome either. In these cases, the simple placing of a hand on the patient's shoulder communicates the warmth of friendship most eloquently.

4. *Have a pleasant facial expression*—a happy countenance and smile can be contagious. A smile commicates warmth and optimism. The patient needs these. On the other hand, foolishness and forced attempts at humor may be upsetting. If the patient feels the pastoral counselor is trying to cheer him up then he might believe he has reason to be depressed or discouraged.

5. *Be brief*—a good visit (like a good prayer) is measured by depth, not length. The quality is much more important than the quantity of the contact. However, the pastoral counselor must not be brusque or hurried if the patient initiates and invites a longer visit. Sensitivity to the patient's emotional needs and physical condition is necessary in determining how long to stay.

6. *Visit when well*—if the pastoral counselor has a cold or sore throat or doesn't feel well, he should not visit at all. Often the patient's resistance to infection is at its lowest when in the hospital.

7. *Remember that the patient's condition is personal*—even though the pastoral counselor may be advised of the patient's diagnosis and prognosis, it is best to let the patient share whatever facts of his condition he feels is relevant to the visit. Whereas one patient may find it helpful to talk about his illness, another may feel embarrassed to do so. It is best to let the patient take the lead.

8. *Consider the patient's rights*—the pastoral counselor should not moralize or take advantage of a captive audience. The patient is likely to have feelings of loss due to hospitalization already and may react adversely if he feels pushed or coerced in any way. A gentle approach will likely be the most effective.

9. *Keep personal problems to yourself*—the patient should not be burdened with the problems of the pastoral counselor in addition to his own. If his personal problems are that pressing, the pastoral counselor should not be in contact with the patient. He is there to help, not receive help.

10. *Eye contact*—sit or stand where eye contact can be made with the patient without making him change position. Also the pastoral counselor should not sit near a light source which will cause a patient discomfort if he looks in that direction.

11. *Always identify yourself*—unless the patient is well known by the pastoral counselor, an introduction should be made early in the conversation. This is only common courtesy and will eliminate any possibility of embarrassing mistakes. Also, the pastoral counselor should not presume any family relationship or other visitors in the patient's room. Wait for an introduction or an acknowledgement of them by the patient. Since many patients are in semi-private rooms, the pastoral counselor should not ignore the roommate of the patient he is visiting. A small courtesy would be to inquire if the roommate's pastor, priest or rabbi has been informed of his admission to the hospital. If not, the pastoral counselor should act as liaison and communicate with the appropriate religious advisor.

12. *Enter the room only if the call light above the door is not on*—the light indicates that the patient needs nursing assistance. It is best to come back later when these needs have been attended. Otherwise, the patient may be on the bedpan

or be in need of a pain shot, and the pastoral counselor cannot establish rapport under these circumstances.

These practical suggestions will make the pastoral counselor's visit more effective. They are small details in some respects but can exert a large influence on the counseling situation. Attention to these points may prevent difficulties in establishing and maintaining an optimum rapport with the hospitalized patient. To this extent, they are part of the skills and tools of the pastoral counselor.

Chapter VI

Moral and Ethical Considerations in Determining the Prolongation of Life

Even before the classic Karen Quinlan case, the issues surrounding the use of indefinite life-sustaining technology were thrust upon physicians and clergymen alike. The pastoral counselor has been called upon to assist families and physicians in making difficult decisions. In order to render the greatest help, the pastoral counselor must be acquainted with many various aspects of this moral dilemma. Often the pastoral counselor will be asked by patient's families when and how much life-sustaining functions should be employed and—most difficult—when they should be withdrawn.

The following discussion is intended to provide a framework upon which moral and ethical considerations may be built. The pastoral counselor should always bear in mind, however, the unique character of each particular situation.

It is apparent that death and dying may be viewed from a variety of perspectives in our present society. More and more, however, attention is being directed toward the degree of human choice which can be morally exercised by those in the dying process.

Thus it is that a patient or a patient's family will opt for all extraordinary measures of sustaining life with no regard for the quality of life, and another patient and/or family choose to discontinue such measures deeming them destructive of personal integrity. Wherever such choice exists, morality and ethics come into play. In order to approach the issues involved, this chapter will probe the essential nature of man and define categories of quality of life; an attempt will be made to quantify the quality of life; and finally, the moral implications of prolonging life with regard to quality of life will be examined.

Since death can be defined as the cessation of life, dying can only be understood if life is comprehended. In a sense, life is a movement toward death, the ultimate destiny (Keleman, 1974). As indicated, human life can be examined from many perspectives, however, an examination of the exact nature of human life is necessary before any taxonomy is attempted.

Defining the Quality of Life

While affirming the wholistic nature of man, it may be helpful to describe, but not define, human life as an equation. The equation is: Body + Mind = Life (Genesis 2:7). Man's body is the means of environmental awareness, and his mind is the vehicle of self-consciousness, and the spirit is the agent of responding to the Divine dimension. A wholistic approach is denoted in the connectional sign (+), and the factors (body, spirit) are separated only to show that the fusion of the physical and the metaphysical (or material and immaterial) is the essence of life. This union is so vital that when either factor is affected, the other is affected necessarily. The various possible inter-relationships between body-health and mind-health are outlined in greater detail in the following paragraphs.

The line of demarcation between life and death is not sharp and simple (Zimring, 1973). There are at least four major degrees of wholeness or combinations of health of body and spirit, plus an infinitesimal number of variations in each category. Probably no two human beings are "alive" in exactly the same way. Further, life, for any individual, is dynamic and not static. Constant movement among the levels of living is expected. This, if nothing else, is due to changes caused by maturation and development.

The first and most obvious category of life is that which might be described as average or "normal." This is the condition in which the body function and the spirit function are clinically described as healthy, and the individual copes satisfactorily in society. Obviously, vast individual differences can be noted physiologically and psychologically and yet each individual is autonomous and self-determining. To be healthy physically and mentally is not only a personal goal and good, but it is a societal goal as well. This category represents the highest level of quality of life.

A second category or level can be constructed in which the person evidences a healthy body, but whose mind is not whole. Thus, the process of accurate self-awareness is impaired within the individual. Such persons are clinically described as mentally ill which, hopefully, may be but a temporary condition of the self. Accordingly, mental retardation is perceived as a developmental slowness or arrest of full self-awareness. In any event, at a given time an individual may be so classed or categorized because he is not able to function satisfactorily in society. He needs outside help and often institutionalization. The quality of life is such that therapy healing is needed; the individual is no longer a fully functioning person. Diagnostic classifications are legion, as vast differences in type and extent of illness are clinically delineated and described.

A third category is that which may be thought of as the reverse of the second. It is comprised of those individuals in whom the mind is whole and healthy, but whose physical body does not function properly. Again, the nature and intensity of the unwholeness involved spans an almost end-less spectrum. As with the second category, an individual's inclusion in this category may be brief and temporary (acute), or it may be of long duration (chronic). At any rate, the degree of sickness is such that institutionalization is usually necessary since the individual cannot cope and func-tion independently. The physical assistance of others is necessary.

It is evident that a single individual can experience each of these first three categories but not simultanteously. As described, they are mutually exclusive. However, the fourth category is that in which the individual combines the nega-tive aspects of both the second and third categories. That is, the individual is sick in mind and body at the same time. This category is the lowest level of quality of life.

Having already defined death as the cessation of life and defining the individual in holistic terms, most individuals "die" when the body becomes so unhealthy because of dis-ease or trauma that it ceases to function at all. However, vital basic functions of the body often can be artificially main-tained for varying periods of time so that the individual can be "kept alive." (Kubler-Ross, 1969). The focus of this discus-sion will be on the heroic means used within the hospital environment. The moral question then arises of when and for how long should such procedures be used. To answer these questions, a discussion of the measurement of these proce-dures and the implications of such measurement follows.

A Quantification of the Quality of Life
This writer (Saylor, 1977) proposes that there are at least four major functions of the physical body which can be artificially maintained. These functions can be outlined and the degree of dependence roughly quantified on a continuum ranging from independence to total dependence. A fifth function, cognition, though not artificially maintained, con-

tributes also to the quantification of the quality of life. It is advanced herein that the greater the degree of dependence, the greater the need for extraordinary or heroic measures to sustain life, thus lowering the over-all quality of life.

Respiration. Total independence on this dimension is simply being able to inhale and exhale unassisted. Partial dependence might include the use of oxygen in order to increase the supply of same to the red blood cells via the lungs. Complete dependence is seen when the individual cannot breathe without a machine such as the positive breathing machine or an iron lung.

Alimentation. Total independnece here would be the ability to take in food with no assistance, or perhaps might include spoon-feeding as well. Partial dependnce could include the use of an I.V. in order to supplement the diet, if the proper kind of quantity of food (or liquid) is not consumed by the individual. Full dependence involves the use of a tube to force-feed the individual who cannot take in any food otherwise.

Elimination. By the same token the ability of the person to eliminate waste can be examined in terms of dependence also. Independence is demonstrated when the individual can use the stool or bedpan with little or no assistance. Partial dependence might be indicated by the necessity of using a catheter to urinate. Complete dependence would be the necessity of using an artificial kidney machine (dialysis) to filter waste products from the blood.

Ambulation. A fourth dimension is the degree to which the individual is self-directive with regard to body movement. Complete independence is the ability to achieve locomotion without any artificial aids or assistance. Partial dependence might include the use of a cane, walker or wheelchair (propelled by the individual himself). Total dependence would be the inability to move the larger skeletal muscles of the lower extremities or full paralysis.

Cognition. Whether or not one conceives of cognition as a physical or psychological event, a fifth index of full function of the person is his mental activity. Although no heroic or body-sustaining measures are involved, three degrees of awareness are suggested which will yield a dependence score. The first is the ability to comprehend and communicate adequately with or without such devices as a hearing aid. The second cognitive level is clinically called confusion in which the individual either perceives or verbalizes inappropriately or both. The third stage is that of no response at all, or coma. The ultimate in lack of response is a level reading on the EEG.

It is proposed then that four indices of physical function and one index of psychological function can be noted, and in each of these there are three levels of dependence which are clinically observable. Realizing the risk of inappropriate quantification and emphasizing that the product obtained is ordinal and not ratio, it can be noted that if the number one (1) is used to represent complete independence, the number two (2) for partial independence and the number three (3) for complete dependence, a score of numerical representation can be obtained. Thus, a completely independent individual would have a score of 5 (1 X 5 indices), and the partially dependent individual would have a score of 10 (2 X 5 indices) and the fully dependent individual would have a score of 15 (3 X 5 indices). (See Figure 2.)

Various combinations ranging from 5 to 15 will indicate the degree of dependence of a given individual, thus, reflecting the quality of life. This system can be illustrated by two hypothetical case histories which follow:

Mrs. T., 80 years old, Caucasian female suffered a massive CVA. After six weeks of hospitalization, the patient is still unconscious, or comatose (D-3, E-3). She is continually on oxygen (A-2) and is tube fed (B-3). Patient was catheterized upon admission and

FUNCTION	1 Complete· Independence	2 Partial Dependence	3 Complete Dependence
A. RESPIRATION	No Assistance	Oxygen needed	On Respirator
B. ALIMENTATION	No Assistance, Spoon-feeding	Intra-venous Nourishment	Tube Feeding
C. ELIMINATION	No Assistance	Catheter needed	Kidney machine needed
D. AMBULATION	No Assistance, Cane	Walker or Wheelchair used	Paralyzed
E. COGNITION	Clear, lucid	Confused at times	No response, comatose

Fig. 2 - Dependency Index

has remained so (C-2). This patient has a
dependence rating of 13 (2 + 3 + 2 + 3 + 3).

Consider another instance:

John A., age 84, Caucasian male was admitted to the
hospital with a diagnosis of hypertension. His blood
pressure was 100/105 and two hours after admission
he suffered an apparent stroke. After six weeks, the
patient still is confused and disoriented (E-2), but can
respond to simple commands. Damage is mainly
confined to left side of body. Patient can walk with
walker and a brace on the left leg (D-2). He is
incontinent (C-2) and must be spoon-fed between
intravenous feedings (B-2). No oxygen is required
(A-1). This patient has a dependence score of 9
(2 + 2+ 2 + 2 + 1).

A comparison of these two composite scores shows how
a general application of the scale can be made. In an institu-
tional setting in which large numbers of patients are involved, such a quantification system can be useful as a brief
descriptive technique which can be easily communicated.
Further refinements in calibration could be made by using
decimal points to indicate increments, such as 1.5, 2.8, etc.

Implications of the Quality of Life

Such a system of quantification has value only in identifying those patients who may be considered for a review of
their quality of life status. Patients with a high score would
presumably be those whose physical body is being maintained by "heroic" efforts alone. Obviously, any decision by
any physician and/or family member to discontinue these
efforts would have to take into account many factors. Such
factors as the age of the patient, the amount of pain the
patient experiences, the expressed (and real) wishes of the
patient's family, previous statements of desire by the patient
(See "A Living Will, Appendix A), medical prognosis and

even the financial burden upon the family. All might be taken into consideration.

No one, physician or family members, wants to "play God" or have any feelings of guilt, doubt or responsibility in making the decision to remove body-sustaining measures. However, the morality involved in continuing procedures that subject the patient to a quality of life that is unacceptable to any rational human being is questionable at best. (Kovarik, 1974) Ultimately, subjective criteria come to bear on the problem. At the risk of seeming very prosaic, it would seem quite appropriate to apply the Golden Rule at this point. A physician and/or family member would have to honestly ask (and answer) the question: "If this were *me* (not my relative), would *I* want to be kept 'alive' in this condition for this period of time?" To do unto others as we would have others do to us may, after all, make the most sense in providing a basis for making this emotionally charged value judgment. As Maguire (1974) notes, ". . . there is an immense difference between deciding on your own death and deciding on the death of another."

Very often a reluctance to discontinue body-sustaining measures is grounded in a sentimentalism which disguises true feelings. It is expressed that it is not morally right to stop these measures once begun, but actually it is a case of not facing the concept of death realistically. It is as though by postponing death, its reality is denied. This is compounded by a fear of anticipated guilt feelings.

Such a decision can be made easier and more accurately, however, if a genuine empathy with the patient is emphasized, not merely an imposition of one's own will upon the patient. (Kubler-Ross, 1974) It should also be emphasized that this is not a prelude to mercy-killing and that only those heroic measures which destroy the integrity and dignity of the individual are in question. Neither should this be interpreted as a substitute for further medical research, as charged by some. (Holleb, 1974 and Ingelfinger, 1974) However, the other alternative is an acceptance of the belief that it is morally right for a human body to be artificially maintained only because it is medically possible to do so.

The morality involved in the issue of the indefinite prolonging of life artificially is contingent upon the definition of death which is employed. Veach (1975), for example, defines death as ". . . the irreversible loss of that which is essentially significant to the nature of man." Maguire (1974) gives a clinically oriented view of death when he declares:

> *"If as a result of an accident, there was clear evidence that the cerebral cortex had been drastically damaged and only the brain stem continued to be functional, it would seem clear that personal life has been extinguished."*

Clearly the cessation of spontaneous respiration and heart-beat are inadequate as ultimate criteria of death. Even the "brain death" concept has not been uniformly embraced or endorsed. How one defines death affects one's moral attitude toward discontinuing mechanical systems that perpetuate a vegetal existence. As Veach (1975) points out:

> *"However, we must also consider that there will be moral infringement if a patient who should be considered dead is considered living . . . This is the harm done to others by treating a human corpse as if it were still a living person."*

On the other hand, it would certainly be immoral to consider as dead a patient who is still living. To discontinue life-sustaining efforts on behalf of the living is as morally reprehensible as continuing those same measures when it is evident that human life is not present. The point is that both situations are ethically unacceptable.

In view of the lack of consensus about the medical definition of death, it is no wonder that the legal ramifications are likewise obfuscated. Thus, the legal aspects of discontinuing heroic treatment of the terminally ill have never been faced directly. However, a brief survey of the litigation which has followed acts of active euthanasia shows that those whose motives are viewed as compassionate are rarely convicted of homicide. In fact, only one conviction of first degree murder has been returned in a total of only twelve cases (Vaughn, 1974).

The moral pivot is not only motive but means. While some would argue that discontinuing body-sustaining measures is the same as active euthanasia (Maguire, 1974; Rachels, 1975), most view the two as being quite different. For example, the AMA position is noted in the following quote from Rachels (1975):

> "The intentional termination of the life of one human being by another—mercy killing – is contrary to that for which the medical profession stands and is contrary to the policy of the American Medical Association."
>
> "The cessation of the employment of extraordinary means to prolong the life of the body when there is irrefutable evidence that biological death is imminent is the decision of the patient and/or his immediate family. The advice and judgment of the physician should be freely available to the patient and/or his immediate family."

Further, the Bishops of the Netherlands affirm the policy of the Roman Catholic Church to be thus (Baughman, et al, 1973):

> "There is no absolute need to prolong indefinitely a life which has been despaired of, by means of medicines and machines, especially if the life in

*question is purely vegetal, without signs of human
reaction. In the latter case above, all extraordinary
means may be omitted and the natural process allowed
to take its course."*

The laws of the Talmud state (Zimring, 1973):

*"We are forbidden to shorten the life of a dying
man by even one moment. But it is also forbidden to
prolong his life artificially when there are no prospects
for him to remain alive."*

So even though the nomenclature involved is not necessarily consistent in the literature, the concept of moral difference is explicit in most writing. As indicated, some use the
terms active and passive euthanasia (Rachels, 1975; Vau-
ghan, 1974); others use the terms euthanasia and anti-
dysthanasia, or euthanasia by omission (Baughman, 1973).
Still others (Fletcher, 1967) see the moral difference expressed
in terms of "cause" and "permit."

Whatever terminology is employed, it is clear that the
indiscriminate and indefinite use of heroic measures of sustaining basic physical functions constitutes a dubious moral
practice at least. The decision to discontinue such measures
when all meaning, beauty, purpose and consciousness of life
is irrevocably ended becomes the more morally defensible
and humanly desirable.

It is, then, in this area that the pastoral counselor can be
of tremendous value in giving support to the family when
difficult decisions must be made. By taking into account the
quality of life, a determination of the morality and ethics of
an individual case may be more readily apparent. Also, the
pastoral counselor may be asked by the patient or family
about making a living will referred to above. Since several
state legislatures (California and New Mexico, for example)
have passed laws allowing these documents to be legally

60

binding, the pastoral counselor may wish to have copies of a living will readily available.

The New Mexico Law, for example, provides in its "Right to Die Act" for the terminally ill minor as well as for an adult, protects and makes known the patient's intentions, protects the physician and hopsital from liability and notes that such a decision is not suicide in terms of life insurance coverage. Further, such documents protect the family from having to make hard choices when guilt might otherwise be incapacitating. The pastoral counselor can help the patient and/or family work through the factors which might influence any decision made.

SECTION TWO

The Influence of Environmental Factors

Chapter VII

Perceptual Distortion of the Hospital Patient

Every pastoral counselor is well aware of the perceptual misconceptions of some patients. Many patients, particularly the geriatric, are disoriented as to time, place and personal identities. Sometimes, however, the perceptual distortions of the patient are not so obvious to the pastoral counselor. Unfortunately, there is often a reluctance on the part of the hospital staff to take the time to relate to this type of patient. Since the patient is mentally confused, it is not thought necessary to display the personal interest one ordinarily accords the patient.

The purpose of this chapter is to explore the occurrence of perceptual distortion of patients in the general hospital setting. Following a definition of the terms and nomenclature involved, this study will be divided into three main sections: (1) the areas of perceptual distortion, (2) the etiology of perceptual distortion, and (3) the implications of this study for the pastoral counselor.

Definitions. As with many psychological and behavioral terms there is no one standard definition of perception. This is partly because psychological processes and systems are created to explain phenomena which are more often implied then directly observed. The various explanations and interpretations are therefore subject to the theoretical orientation of the observer and are filtered through the past experiences and any subjective biases he might have.

A further complication in defining perception is the relation of sensation to perception. One school of thought conceives of the two elements being quite separable. For instance, separate titles of the Foundations of Modern Psychology Series include a volume, *Sensory Psychology* (Mueller), and another volume entitled, *Perception* (Hochberg). Other psychologists conceive of perception and sensation as fused together as a single unitary system (Cratty, 1970).

For our purpose here, perception will be defined and used as the individual's interpretation of the neural input which their sense organs transmit to the central nervous system. It is thus a subjective, directly unobservable, electrochemical process. Perception can be technically but not actually divorced from sensation which is the objective, mechanical stimulation of the organism's sensorium.

Obviously, the two processes interact, but each can be experienced without the other. That is, it is possible for the organism to perceive in the absence of objective sensory input, as in hallucination. Also, it is possible for the organism *not* to perceive in the presence of sensory input, as in anesthesia. Further, it is possible to translate sensory experience from one sensory mode to another, as in synasthesia.

With these acknowledged restrictions of the general definition offered above, perceptual distortion will be defined as the inaccurate interpretation of sensory data (input). Perceptual distortion as used herein is similar to the clinical concepts of hallucination, delusion, disorientation, and confusion. Perceptual distortion is erroneous perception which is idiosyncratic, highly personalized and is not necessarily tied to objective sensory input.

66

I. Areas of Perceptual Distortion

As definitions of perception are subject to wide variation, so are efforts to categorize or otherwise classify perceptions. Some classifications include at least the five primary senses, vision, audition, touch, taste and smell. Gibson (1966), for example, generally stays with five basic sensations. His categorization of perception is: (1) basic orienting system (forces of gravity, vestibular), (2) auditory system, (3) haptic system (touch), (4) taste-smell, and (5) visual.

Keeping in mind the hospital setting, the area of perceptual distortion extends beyond the so-called five senses. Perceptual distortion is herein examined in three separate areas:

1. Perceptual distortion of the sensory apparatus (visual, auditory, tactile, gustatory and olfactory).

2. Perceptual distortion of pain mechanism.

3. Perceptual distortion of time and body-image.

This particular taxonomy is proposed by the writer in both its selection and arrangement.

1. *Perceptual distortion of the sensory apparatus.* Only brief explanation is necessary at this point. Most, if not all, basic approaches to perception include a discussion of these perceptions with varying degrees of emphasis. Some works are devoted entirely to visual perception, for example. While vision has probably been reported upon most thoroughly, work has been done and is continuing in all areas of sensory perception. Thus, no further attention or amplification will be offered here, except to note that perceptual distortion may occur in each of the various modalities in varying degree.

2. *Perceptual distortion of pain.* It can be argued that a separate classification for pain is unnecessary and redundant. This position is taken by von Fieandt (1966) who conceives of pain as being simply the result of exceeding the

threshold of any of the sensory perceptions. He writes: ". . . pain is considered to be solely a result of stimulation at high intensities, i.e., intensities which exceed the upper threshold or the stimulus maximum. Whatever modality is involved, a maximal stimulus intensity would always produce sensations of pain." This theory of pain can be viewed as an example of pattern theory. Thus, sounds in excess of the toleration limit would produce perceived pain in the hearing sense, etc.

A new theory of pain has been advanced by Melzak and Wall (1965). They propose a "gate control theory of pain." According to this theory, (1) the substantia gelatinosa in the dorsal horn, (2) the dorsal-column fibers that project toward the brain, and (3) the first central transmission (T) cells in the dorsal horn, function, respectively, as (1) the gate control system (2) the central control trigger, and (3) activate the neural mechanisms which comprise the action system responsible for response and perception. They state: "Our theory propose that pain phenomena are determined by interactions among these three systems."

Although their orientation is basically medical, they conclude: "The model suggests that psychological factors such as past experience, attention, and emotion influence pain response and perception by acting on the gate control system." (Melzak and Wall, 1965). The point is made that one's perception of pain involves psychical as well as physical components and is thus subject to distortion as are the primary senses.

The emotional element in pain perception is echoed also in the following: "The emotional reaction to the pain determines the degree of suffering experienced. Physiological processes and anatomical structures provide the substrate for the emotional reaction too, but past experiences stored in these structures are the reference against which the new stimulus is evaluated to determine the emotional reaction." (Eckenhoff, 1968).

These findings are reinforced by clinical observation by any of the hospital staff, including the pastoral counselor.

3. *Perceptual distortion of time and body-image.* The division of this proposed taxonomy is necessitated because these perceptions are different from those arising from identifiable sense organs and also from those perceptions of pain arising from a combination of physical and psychical structures. This third and last classification is unique and warranted because, strictly speaking, no specific, single physical apparatus is directly involved in the perception of time and body-image. These perceptions are mainly psychical and they are intimately related to the environment in which the organism exists, in this case, the hospital.

Even though our physical bodies are the loci and focus of our perceived body-image, it is the reaction of significant others in our environment which supplies us with the perceptions about our bodies. This is particularly true since most physical attributes occur on a continuum and their evaluation is a relative and cultural function. In addition, the perception of one's body-image, is related to what his body can actually do. As Cratty (1970) expresses it: ". . . problems related to body image revolved around the relationships between body build and/or the child's perceptions of the acceptability of his body and other psychological and social attributes."

Hospitalization and the illness which precipitates it produce perceptual distortion of both time and body-image. The pastoral counselor may visit many patients who demonstrate the syndrome characteristic of this disequilibrium.

II. Etiology of Perceptual Distortion

Having defined the concepts related to perceptual distortion and set up a proposed taxonomy, the conditions, especially as they related to the hospital environment, under which it occurs will now be examined. In this discussion, five sources of causes will be mentioned. No claim is made to all-inclusiveness; those mentioned would simply seem to be the most obvious.

1. *Cerebral Insufficiency.* One of the major causes of perceptual disorientation is basically physical. The medical term "delirium" is applied to the syndrome in which "illusions, such as misinterpreted visual or auditory stimuli, are not uncommon." (Arieti, 1959). Several common organic conditions lead to its development. These include infections of the central nervous system such as meningitis and encephalitis, and systemic infections such as diphtheria and pneumonia. Exhaustive conditions such as post-surgery and extreme fatigue, which include stress and isolation are likewise involved. Anemia and reduced blood flow to the brain are implicated also.

Three stages or types of delirium have been indicated: initial delirium, febrile delirium (with accompanying fever) and post-febrile delirium (after the fever subsides). Concerning the type and intensity of perceptual distortion involved in delirium, Ebaugh and Tiffany note: "Both the content and severity of the delusions and hallucinations fluctuate considerably from time to time." (Arieti, 1959).

A good deal of the work on delirium has been done by Engel and Romano (1959). Regarding the scope of this organic etiology of mental disturbance, they claim ". . . that many seriously ill hospitalized patients experience some degree of delirium during the course of their illness." The effect of delirium upon perception is noted in the following: "Not only does one have difficulty in focusing attention on the important percept, but one also has difficulty in screening out interferring perceptions, whether they arise from the external environment or from within." They describe several stages of dilirium and conclude that as the condition advances . . . he (the delirious patient) manifests confusion in his orientation as to place, misidentifying his location, or identifying it correctly only by the most painstaking visual search to establish landmarks. He now may misidentify what he perceives, mistaking voices in the hall of those of familiar persons or pieces of furniture for people." (Engel and Romano, 1959).

While emphasizing an organic etiology, they indicate that fluctuations in the manifestations may be due to psychological factors such as the hospital environment as well.

Another facet of organic etiology which can be mentioned without reference to a particular disease is the effect of fever *per se* on perception. In commenting on time perception, von Fieandt notes: "In high fever, time appears faster, which can be shown, for example, by having fever patients count numbers in a prescribed rhythm . . . Compared with physical time, phenomenal time varies widely. Attitudes and expectations play a decisive role. Waiting times are generally long."

2. *Sensory monotony*. Another contributing cause of perceptual distortion in the hospital environment is sensory monotony. Recently, experiments (reported in Forgus, 1964) have been conducted showing that sensory deprivation can dramatically affect perception. This, in combination with isolation, can be responsible for perceptual distortion. Research at McGill University and also at Wright Air Force Base supports the following conclusion: "These investigations have indicated that decrements in performance and various abnormal phenomena may occur. Concentration, ability to carry on organized activity, and various intellectual tasks were adversely affected. Visual, aural, and tactual hallucinations were reported." (Forgus, 1964).

Although rigidly controlled experiments in a hospital setting are not feasible, it can be inferred with integrity that hospitalization itself may be a contributing factor in sensory monotony and/or deprivation. As such it may be responsible for fluctuations in perceptual distortion. The kinesthetic restriction imposed by the use of catheters, levines, I.V.'s transfusion, etc., to say nothing of traction, leg and body casts, etc., and the standard isolation room procedures all are no doubt in some part contributory. Added to these medical considerations are the often monotonous room colors and decoration and the absence of clocks and calendars in rooms, and poor lighting. Small wonder patients sometimes appear to be confused and unresponsive. As Combs and Snygg (1959) put it: "When an individual is sick enough to be confined to his bed, it is easy for us to understand how his abilities to perceive may be restricted by his inability to get around."

3. *Emotional stress.* The trauma of illness and hospitalization can result in heightened emotionality and anxiety which, in turn, can be responsible for perceptual distortion. The subject to how the sick perceive the world has been well documented. According to Lederer (1952), the sick person experiences three stages of illness: (1) the transition period from health to illness, (2) the period of "accepted" illness and, (3) convalescence.

After a person accepts illness, he regresses to a state of dependence similar to that of childhood. His self-perception changes from when he was well. As Lederer (1952) says: "Like a child, the patient often exhibits an uncritical 'love' and admiration for his benefactors but at the same time resentment toward them because of his weak and inferior relation to them. All persons working with the sick should anticipate and learn to recognize his ambivalent dependency and neither be flattered, nor offended by it." The period of convalescence is likened to adolescence. In this stage, the patient often reacts by wrenching loose from the pattern of dependency he has known. He is in a great hurry to recuperate, and may prematurely dismiss his physician and overextend his physical strength.

Hospitalization may bring forth hidden anxieties concerning the patient's body-image. Even the temporary loss of function of a body part may set the stage for perceptual distortion. Schoenberg, et al, (1970) express it well: "The body-image has an integrity and intactness which are presumed to reflect basic aspects of one's ego integration. When this integration is weak, disruption of the body-image through surgery or amputation may precipitate blatant psychotic or delusional behavior."

Add to this the emotionality of perhaps an ambulance ride and the cold sterility of the emergency room, and it is easy to understand the patient's confusion which often results.

4. *Hallucinogens.* Since the influence of drugs on perception is the subject of much current investigation, no elaboration of this facet of perceptual distortion will be made here. Obviously, many drugs prescribed by physicians and dispensed from hospital pharmacies come under this category. Patients may experience perceptual distortion in a hospital setting due to the somewhat routine use of anesthetic and pain reducing procedures.

5. *Special cases.* Most pastoral counselors have had experience in dealing with the perceptual distortion known as the phantom limb phenomenon. This is the perception of pain in the amputated limb, and its occurrence has been attributed to both organic and psychological etiology. Current surgical techniques have minimized the organic origins of the phenomenon.

6. *Paralysis of the lower extremities.* Another special instance of perceptual distortion has been noted in hemiplegia, Burt (1970) writes: "With the changes in the tactile sense, there may be a unilateral loss of the sense of touch, illusions

or hallucinations of touch may develop, or touch on the affected side." The similarity of this with the phantom limb phenomenon is apparent. Assumedly, the same neural and psychological mechanisms are involved.

Having discussed the etilogical aspects of perceptual distortion in the hospital environment, it remains only to deal with the implications of this study for the pastoral counselor.

III. Implications For The Pastoral Counselor

The implications of this study for the pastoral counselor are several. First of all, the recognition of the syndrome and clinical features should give the pastoral counselor an understanding of the behavior associated with perceptual distortion. For example, to realize that such behavior (as in the case of delirium) is not to be taken as uncooperative or hostile but is a step in giving such a patient that consideration and assurance he desperately needs.

This leads to a second implication and that is that the pastoral counselor, as a member of the healing team, can assist the patient in correcting his perceptual disorientation. The pastoral counselor, in his personal contacts, can help to calm and allay the fears and anxiety which are expressed by the patient. In a non-punitive role, the pastoral counselor can kindly but firmly help the patient re-orient himself in a strange and hostily perceived hospital environment. By the support of his presence, the pastoral counselor can be a living bridge to the world of reality.

Another important implication of this study is to indicate the importance of the pastoral counselor relating to a patient in isolation. By entering the patient's perceptual field, the pastoral counselor can help relieve the sensory monontony often characteristic of isolation procedures. By his physical presence and by his drawing out the patient, the pastoral counselor can help stimulate the patient and thus help him avoid the conditions which otherwise might aggravate the onset of perceptual distortion.

As in many other instances, the pastoral counselor's relationship to the patient's family can be very significant. By assuring them that the perceptual distortion may be only temporary and symptomatic or helping them deal with its permanency, the patient's family can more effectively visit and help reduce the anxiety that the patient already has. It may be necessary to communicate these aspects of the patient's condition to other visitors as well as his family.

Finally, the pastoral counselor may assist by reporting changes in the patient's behavior that he observes in his contacts. Since the clinical features of delirium, for example, do not manifest themselves on a continuing, predictable basis, the pastoral counselor can note instances when the symptoms are present and simply convey it verbally to the nurse or physician.

Chapter VIII

Patients' Perceptions of the Hospital

In order to appreciate fully the patient's perceptual field, the pastoral counselor should be aware of the impact that hospitalization, per se, has on the patient. To do this, it is necessary to examine several factors which influence patients' perceptions in order to understand and deal with these perceptions. The purpose of this chapter is to examine three large areas of patients' perceptions: (1) their pereceptions of loss in hospitalization, (2) their perceptions of hospital personnel, and (3) their perceptions of hospital policy. The following observations would seem to apply to most hospitals regardless of size or geographical location.

Many people have a negative image and a disproportionate fear of hospitalization (Larson, 1971). Generally speaking, the patient comes to the hospital with a mixture of anger and embarrassment. Our society is youth oriented in which only the old are sick. One who is hospitalized often sees his role as that of the inferior and is angry at the role of dependency he must adopt. Further, there may be a sense of embarrassment due to the very nature of anatomical location of his illness. Persons often are reluctant to enter and in a hurry to leave the hospital.

I. Patients' Perceptions of Loss

Apart from the physical pain and financial strain that hospitalization implies, this phobic reaction to hospitalization may be a function of the patient's perception of loss. Just as there is a psychological grief process occasioned by the death and loss of a significant person, there is a similar response set in motion by the perceptions of loss in the hospitalization process. Some problem patient behavior in the hospital, such as hostility to staff, may possibly be explained in this light (Williams, 1974).

It is suggested herein that there are at least three different classes or categories of loss as perceived by the hospitalized patient. These are not exhaustive in breadth or depth, but they will serve to illustrate the basic premise.

1. *Information-giving as loss.* The very admitting procedure is threatening to some patients. Being asked to divulge information relative to age, marital status or religious preference, may produce a defensive reaction in the respondent. Men as well as women are self-conscious about their age. Neither sex wishes to be implicitly reminded they are growing older. Similarly, if a person has just come through a messy divorce procedure, the very mention of marital status may trigger a host of unpleasant emotional associations. Also, a person's religious affiliation may be considered a very private matter, and he may perceive the question as an attack on his existing value system.

This is to say nothing about the questions concerning the financial arrangements the patient has made to settle his account. Questions as to place or type of employment and the number and coverage of whatever health insurance policies are possessed are potentially emotion-producing queries. The symbolic as well as real significance of one's resources play a definite part in the patient's attitude toward his hospitalization. A person's fear as to what might become of his vacated position at work while he is in the hospital may well add to his anxiety and be reflected in a reluctance to enter and a rush to depart (Vollicer, 1973).

78

The intent of these standard queries may be negatively interpreted by the extremely sensitive patient who is already in a state of heightened emotionality. In order to defuse this potentially upsetting experience, the pastoral counselor should try to make contact with the patient as soon as possible following admission. He can actually begin the therapeutic process the patient needs by interpreting various aspects of the admitting procedure. Too often an impersonal, mechanical approach by any hospital personnel results in the patient's perception of loss and actually increases the apprehension which the patient likely already possesses. The pastoral counselor can help reverse these perceptions by demonstrating a genuine concern for the patient's feelings at this point.

2. *Lack of Control or Loss.* For obvious reasons, the incoming patient does not choose his ward or room. Hopefully, a measure of choice is given as to whether the roommate smokes or not. By and large, however, his assignment will depend on room availability and his diagnosis (Smith, 1976). Also, he will have no control as to meal times and often substitutes are made in the menu he does select. For some diagnostic procedures, he may have to skip a meal entirely.

The patient will be cautioned against keeping any money or valued possessions with him. This is likely to be interpreted as loss occasioned by hospitalization, since money and possessions symbolize power and control. He likewise loses control over his time and schedule. Our society is very time oriented, but a patient is put into a room usually without either clock or calendar. From being a self-directive person, the patient is suddenly cast from an active into a passive role. He perceives himself at the mercy of capricious nurses who take his vital signs and administer drugs and injections on a schedule he is at a loss to understand, much less control.

One of the more threatening losses a patient experiences is the lack of control over his own body (Pike, 1975). His physical anatomy is surrendered when he is confined to bed rest with no bathroom privileges, as being in traction, or when anesthesia is administered prior to surgery. This is to say nothing of the physical restrictions occasioned by the almost ubiquitous intravenous tubes in the patient's arm or any of the different encumbering devices known as catheters, levines, etc. As each constricting and restricting therapeutic measure is added, the level of anxiety may well escalate proportionately.

3. *Lack of Knowledge as Loss.* Probably the most devastating loss any patient experiences is the lack of knowledge. This occurs whenever the patient feels that information relative to his diagnosis or prognosis is not being adequately communicated to him (Levitt, 1975). Often, the larger the institution, the more difficult communication becomes. Results of routine tests may be slow in getting to the patient's chart for a myriad of reasons. Meanwhile, the patient's imagination runs rampant and he envisions dreadful and dire complications.

Sometimes the physician's attitude toward his patients is such that he feels that patients cannot constructively handle even the most elementary medical information. More probably, the information gleaned from a routine test shows nothing of significance and nothing is told the patient because there is "nothing to tell." Other physicians prefer to wait until a whole battery of tests are administered and evaluated. Meanwhile, the patient feels ignored and neglected. Physicians and nurses tend to forget how important to the patient bits of information really are.

There is some debate as to whether and how much bad news should be conveyed to the patient and/or his family. Inasmuch as most patients will interpret the withholding of information as negative (often to unrealistic proportions), it seems that the lack of knowledge is more emotionally threatening than an honest sharing of pertinent information.

Lack of knowledge is perceived as loss by the patient whenever communication is impaired at any level of his care. Not knowing how to turn on the television set in his room may be almost as frustrating as not knowing when his next pill is due. The amount of time spent in explaining or entertaining the patient's questions will be to the patient's emotional state beneficial and economical to the physician's and nurse's time (Pike, 1975).

II. Patient's Perceptions of Hospital Personnel

Similarly, patients' perceptions of the personnel may contribute to the negative image which hospitalization often projects. Since hospitalization involves relating to people whose emotional affect is heightened by whatever brings them to the hospital, hospital personnel are more prone to be perceived in an undesirable light, rather than either favorable or neutral.

This potential for personality conflict is complicated by the fact that hospital personnel are not primarily educated and equipped to deal with the intense feelings of many hospital patients. Hospital personnel are well trained in the scientific method in various medical specialties, but their training seldom involves a strong emphasis on the behavioral sciences ("Patients' Days," 1976). This being the case, their understanding of interpersonal relationships is more often the product of trial and error methodology. Usually an acquaintance with personality theory, *per se*, is more accidental than intentional.

Three groups of hospital personnel will be reviewed here as being the most visible and obvious. These are the physician, nurse and technician. However, the patient's perception of hospitalization will also be influenced by other hospital personnel such as housekeepers, maintenance workers, etc., insofar as they have patient contact.

1. *Physicians.* Though the physician is not a hospital employee as such as his or her contact with the patient may be relatively brief compared to the nurses', the patient's perception of the physician should not be overlooked. If the patients are satisfied with their physician, their perception of their hospitalization may well be more favorable. The converse is also true. If the patient feels frustrated because his physician is not as attentive as desired, some of this frustration is likely to be projected upon other hospital personnel. Some hospital patients deify their physician to the extent that they are not able to express adequately their anger or fears directly. However, other members of the hospital staff are not invulnerable.

As indicated, a common patient perception of the physician is that of an extremely powerful person who controls the patients' physical destiny. Patients who so regard their physician find it difficult to accept disappointment when their recovery is not as swift or complete as desired. They may internalize their anger and frustration at not getting well and feel their continued lack of progress is their own fault.

Another unwholesome patient perception of their physician is that which perceives the physician as just the opposite. They perceive the various test procedures and medications ordered as basically experimental. The hospital patient perceives himself as the "guinea pig." Such a perception may be a projection, a defense mechanism which is designed (as when the physician is deified) to place all responsibility for lack of recovery outside himself. This perception divests the patient of the anxiety of not doing his part in the therapeutic process.

In either case, faulty perceptions of the physician's powers can result in a disillusioned and thereby difficult hospital patient.

2. *Nurses.* The patients' perception of the nursing staff will be greatly influenced by their perception of their physician. The nurse will be closely identified with the physician as an authority figure. However, most patients perceive the nurse as somewhat less powerful than the doctor and thereby more human and approachable. Generally, this means that the nurse will come into more verbal abuse than the physician and more demands will be made upon the nursing staff.

Because of the frequency of contact, the nurse may well become the most significant person during the patient's hospitalization. However, the hospitalized patient's perception of the nurse is somewhat ambivalent. At one and the same time the nurse is an angel of mercy and the clinical disciplinarian. These perceptions are antithetic and the patient shifts perceptions easily depending upon their perceived needs of the moment.

In this context, it is easy to see how conflicts between nurse and patient might arise. The nurse will probably not have a self-image as ambivalent as the patient's perception. For example, the patient whose dominate perception of the nurse is that of an angel of mercy may quickly run counter to her perceived self-image as clinical disciplinarian and vice-versa.

3. *Technicians.* Most hospitals have an increasingly specialized cadre of technicians. These include such hospital staff members as respiratory therapists, physical therapists, lab technicians and X-ray technicians. The patients' perceptions of these hospital technicians varies according to the amount of contact between them. In some cases, the exposure to technicians is brief and cursory. In other cases, such as that between the orthopedic patient and the physical therapist, the relationship might be very intense.

Generally, the hospital patient perceives the technician as less powerful than the physician and nurse. However, as in the case of the orthopedic patient, the amount of time spent and the perceived good from that contact may result in the technician being a more significant person than either.

Technicians tend to be perceived in a negative way since most of their contact with the patient is pain-producing. The lab technician who draws blood, the X-ray technician who makes the patient lie in uncomfortable positions, the respiratory therapist who urges the patient to blow harder into the breathing machine, and the physical therapist who makes a patient walk on a painful limb—all these contacts with the patient may be somewhat painful though these procedures are obviously necessary and therapeutic.

Also since the technician is perceived less powerful than the physician or nurse, he may come into more verbal abuse from the patient. At the same time, because he does seem more approachable, the technician may actually enjoy a better rapport with the patient.

Other hospital personnel who contribute to the patients' overall perception of hospitalization are persons like the admitting clerks, housekeepers, maintenance men, et al. Often there is a need for their awareness of the potential impact of their limited contact with the patient, too. Each personal contact may affect favorably or unfavorably the patients' perceptions of the hospitalization process. The pastoral counselor, hopefully, can favorably influence patients' perceptions by showing a genuine concern for the patient as a person and also as an object of God's love and care.

III. Patients' Perceptions of Hospital Policy

In addition to patients' perceptions of loss and of hospital personnel, their perceptions of hospital procedure are important in their over-all attitude toward hospitalization (Corbus and Connell, 1974). Their perceptions are derived and distilled from their composite experience. Variations that exist between different types of hospitals (private, federal, community, etc.) and different kinds of hospitals (general, pediatric, maternity, etc.) are amalgamated into a generalized, global perception of what being in the hospital means. The impact of these perceptions in three selected facets of hospital procedure will be noted below.

1. *Financial Policy.* Patients' perceptions of the hospitals financial policy are often ambiguous. Often the patient is not sure whether the hospital is an institution of mercy or simply another member of the business community. Few hospitals are so endowed that their financial policy can be very lenient. At the same time, Hill-Burton recipient institutions cannot refuse service to those unable to pay. Patients' perceptions of a hospital's financial policy will be influenced also by stories of people dying because a given hospital wouldn't admit them because of financial inability. Also instances of hospital bills being turned over to a professional collection agency will color a patient's attitude toward the hospital's fiscal policy (Larson, 1971).

Another factor which influences patients' perceptions of hospital financial policy is the patient's physical condition. The heightened emotionality of a life-threatening illness may make a patient very defensive. The patient may perceive the hospital's legitimate concern for responsibility of payment as proof and evidence that he will not survive the hospitalization. The patients' preoccupation with his own health concerns may make him somewhat paranoid and fearful.

Too often patients become cynical about hospital costs because they do not have any conception of the financial pressures which are brought to bear upon today's hospital. They perceive "someone is getting rich" at their expense and that great financial profit is being realized in direct proportion to human suffering. If the patient is billed too soon after discharge, the hospital is "greedy;" if he is billed too long after discharge, the hospital is "inefficient."

85

2. *Security Policy*. Depending somewhat upon such geographic factors as size of community and hospital location, security is a definite part of hospital policy. Whether the concern is petty theivery from patient rooms or mugging in the parking lot, most hospitals have at least an implicit security policy. The patients' perceptions of these policies will probably vary according to previous hospital experience. The patient who lost some personal article may be very critical of the security policy. Others with no previous problems may feel that the presence of armed and uniformed security guards is an unjustified expenditure of hospital funds.

Related to the overall security policy of the hospital are the parking and visitor policies. Patients often perceive these as impediments to their families and fail to appreciate the rationale behind these policies (Pike, 1975). They may well perceive these policies as designed solely for the convenience of the hospital staff and further evidence of the insensitivity of the hospital to their comfort. Patients and visitors alike may perceive enforced visiting hours as being unnecessarily harsh and restrictive.

Also involved here are the fire and safety procedures. Sometimes even the routine fire drill may be perceived by the patient as an unnecessary nuisance. Policies devised to insure patient safety, such as use of wheelchairs to transfer or discharge ambulatory patients, may also be perceived by the patient as hospital inefficiency instead of genuine regard for their well-being. The entire hospital staff, including the pastoral counselor, should be alert to interpret correctly hospital policies that are misunderstood by the patient.

3. *Administrative Policies*. In a sense, all hospital policies are administrative in that the administration implements them. However, such policies as staffing ratio, replacing equipment, and plant utilization are examples of those which are more clearly administrative rather than departmental. The patients' perceptions that the hospital is

understaffed or overstaffed, that hospital equipment is out-moded or modern, and that more or less space should be used for patient lounges or whatever are based on administrative-level decisions and policy.

Depending on the size of the hospital and the personal philosophy of the administration, most administrators keep a low profile in regard to direct patient contact. For this reason, patients' perception of administrative policies are seldom verbalized. This is not saying that the perceptions do not exist. Part of the patients' overall perception of hospitalization will be strongly influenced by administrative policies. Patients' perceptions that the hospital is "well run" or efficiently managed will be a reflection of administrative policy and implementation of same.

In the final analysis, the buck stops at the administrator's desk. So the patient's perception of administrative policy well may be the cumulative effect of the entire hospitalization experience. Hospitals, like people, have personalities all their own. The reputation a given institution maintains will often be a reflection, more clear than distorted, of its administration.

This consideration of patients' perceptions of the hospitalization process also emphasizes the discrepancy between the values society at large reinforces and those which the hospital society reinforces. The dimension on which this is most obvious is that of independence. Whereas the one encourages and rewards initiative and self-actualization, the other may tend to encourage and reward passivity and dependence. Far too often the ideal or model patient is the docile person who surrenders a measure of his self-integrity. Those in the caring and healing professions are often guilty of fostering this attitude in the name of benevolent management (Cousins, 1976).

IV. Conclusion

Perceptions that patients develop toward hospitalization are the result of many different factors interacting with each patients' psychological make-up. These perceptions are complex and capable of shifting. Hospital personnel can be instrumental in shaping these perceptions in a more favorable direction only if they are aware of the processes by which they are generated and sustained.

Such an awareness of the many subtle ways in which perceptions arise in the patient's mind had been the focus of this paper. It is hoped that a heightened realization of the important contribution various hospital procedures, personnel and policies make in the formation of patients' perceptions will be a continued and expanded pursuit of those involved in the delivery of health care.

The pastoral counselor, in his dealing with patients, is in a good position to help uncover misunderstandings of financial, security and administrative policy. Since he also relates to many of the hospital personnel in various contexts, he can help in three specific ways: (1) He can interpret accurately the hospital policies and personnel actions to the patient. (2) He can help the patient understand the interpersonal relationship problems that arise in the hospital environment and how the patient himself relates to them. (3) He can assume the role of the patients' advocate when hospital personnel do err or when hospital policy needs to be changed.

The uniqueness of his position of being familiar with both the hospital milieu and patients' needs gives the pastoral counselor an interested objectivity which is valuable to the hospital and to the patient.

Chapter IX

The Pastoral Counselor and the Hospital Staff

The effectiveness of the pastoral counselor in the hospital setting is greatly enhanced by a good, professional relationship with all the hospital staff. This includes hospital staff at all levels, in all departments. Depending upon the size of the institution, he may not be able to become as well acquainted as he might wish. However, a working relationship with the nursing staff and medical staff is essential for a genuine team approach. This chapter will note several specific ways by which such inter-relatedness can be productive for the benefit of the patient.

The Nursing Staff. Granted that many, if not most, nurses have a deep, personal religious faith and commitment, she usually does not see her role as that of a spiritual adviser. This is part of the "why" of the pastoral counselor. Initially, the nurse may have some anxiety concerning the function of the pastoral counselor and view his presence and ministry in the hospital with some degree of apprehension.

Since pastoral counseling is a relatively new area of specialization, the chapter will attempt to set forth some guidelines which may help the nurse and the pastoral counselor help each other in their common task of patient care. There are at least five ways in which the nurse can best utilize the pastoral counselor's services.

1. *The nurse can acknowledge him as a member of the healing team*. This means that the nurse's attitude toward the pastoral counselor is one of acceptance. His purpose and presence in the patient's room is to complement and supplement the physical care that is being given. His professional training is geared toward the health of the whole man, using the spiritual therapy of Scripture and prayer.

Obviously, the pastoral counselor's ministry to the patient is never intended to supercede or contradict that of the nurse. The pastoral counselor will indeed respect the nurse's role and defer to her and the physician and their schedules. However, the pastoral counselor needs the nurse's respect for his work also. Respect for the role of the pastoral counselor implies that his visits will not be interrupted except as necessary, and that such information be given him in order to assist him in helping to meet the patient's spiritual needs. This leads to the second way in which the nurse can help the pastoral counselor do his job.

2. *The nurse can supply information to the pastoral counselor of unusual aspects of the patient's situation*. A typical instance may help clarify this point. Recently, in our hospital, the pastoral counselor was making a call on the OB unit. As usual, he checked at the nurses station and was advised that one of the new mothers on his list had lost her baby shortly before he arrived. This did two things: it prevented the pastoral counselor from issuing forth with the usual hearty "congratulations," and it enabled him to organize some thought of comfort for the mother. In this particular instance, the only channel of communication for the pastoral counselor was the nurse.

This line of communication to be effective must be reciprocal. The pastoral counselor should, of course, note and relate to the nurse such information that will serve the best interest of the patient. Since a nurse cannot possibly be in all patients' rooms simultaneously and continually, the pastoral counselor can assist by conveying significant aspects of a patient's behavior to the nurse. Whatever makes for good communication assists the nurse-pastoral counselor relationship.

3. *The nurse can suggest a special visit by the pastoral counselor when the patient's situation so indicates.* This information can be in the form of a suggestion to the patient of the pastoral counselor's services and his availability, or the nurse can contact the pastoral counselor directly herself. When should the nurse call the pastoral counselor? Several instances seem to present themselves. Certainly in time of imminent expiration the pastoral counselor should be notified. Whenever a patient's physical condition deteriorates rapidly and vital signs are weakening, the pastoral counselor can be of service and give support to the patient and to the patient's family. Often the patient is not responsive nearing expiration, but usually at this time, the patient's family is near and especially needs the spiritual counseling the pastoral counselor is trained to give.

Even when the prognosis is favorable, the pastoral counselor may be needed by a patient. For example, if the patient is depressed either because of his own condition or because of family problems, the pastoral counselor can bring an understanding and listening ear. He can encourage the patient to ventilate his feelings, and by non-punitive acceptance, he can help the patient work through his discouragement.

There still persists in the thinking of many patients the belief that their illness is somehow a punishment or judgment from God. This attitude may work against the patient's recovery and well-being. By assuring the patient of God's love and grace, the pastoral counselor may help bring the patient to an acceptance of his illness with a more wholesome and constructive attitude.

91

Other instances of the patient's need for the pastoral counselor may include pre-surgical anxiety and postoperative depression. In any time of emotional trauma, the presence and ministry of the pastoral counselor can give support that will aid in the adjustment of the patient.

4. *The nurse can acquaint the aides and student nurses with the services offered by the pastoral counselor.* This awareness includes not only the chapel location and time of services, but should also encompass the counseling ministry which the pastoral counselor provides. Especially if the aide has no regular spiritual adviser or if the student nurse is some distance from her home community, the pastoral counselor can be of direct assistance. By helping with personal problems which may inhibit their effectiveness with the patient, the pastoral counselor offers a valuable service. The pastoral counselor's training and experience in the hospital environment may also help to resolve problems which arise as a result of inter-personal relationships in the ward.

5. *The nurse can assist the pastoral counselor by accepting him as a person as well as a professional.* Although the pastoral counselor speaks to and for the Divine, he lives in a temple of clay like everyone else. He brings to his work and ministry a thoroughly human personality with all the faults and irksome traits common to humanity. He gets uptight and scared at times; he will get too emotionally involved with the patient at times; he will get angry and lose his temper at times. The pastoral counselor takes his work seriously, but he also has a sense of humor. A smile and greeting from the nurse may help make his day.

These areas of assistance are not exhaustive. Each hospital and health care institution has its own philosophy of meeting the religious needs of the patient. As any program develops, there will be changes in the *modus operandi*. However, the essence of the points mentioned above will increase the usefulness of the pastoral counselor's service.

The Medical Staff. The demands on the physician's time and attention are so many that he must often avail himself of various auxiliary services. Such personnel are able to assist the doctor in the hospital setting, and can enable him to give more time to the tasks for which he is specifically trained. The nurse is probably the most easily recognized hospital staff member who renders a great deal of help to the attending physician. Likewise the physical therapist, lab technician, respiratory therapist, and many others contribute to expeditious patient care and recovery. Often overlooked are the services which a pastoral counselor can perform. Some of the ways in which he can relate to and aid the physician will be the focus of this discussion.

The pastoral counselor can be likened to a piece of lab equipment in that his value increases in proportion to its use. Therefore, enough cannot be said relative to the importance of good communication between physician and the pastoral counselor. This is particularly important since many of the services which the pastoral counselor offers are difficult to quantify. He often deals in theological constructs and abstractions as well as scientific fact. So the better the physician knows of the pastoral counselor and the scope of his work, the more the physician can avail himself of his services. Several of these services will now be mentioned; no evaluative ranking is intended in the order of their presentation.

1. *Interpretation.* One significant aspect of the work of the pastoral counselor is in helping to interpret the physician's therapeutic program to the patient. Often the patient's emotional involvement in his illness makes it difficult to "hear" what the physician says. Sometimes the very nature of the severity of the patient's condition is not comprehended by the patient even though the doctor carefully explains it and repeats it. This is not an implied criticism of the physician's approach, but a simple recognition of the patient's

anxiety. The pastoral counselor can help by working through with the patient what the physician has already told the patient.

The pastoral counselor is not trying to "play" doctor or psychiatrist and in no way assumes a medical or psychiatric role. He does, however, listen carefully to the patient and reflect back to him the information which the physician has given. This can conserve the physician's time which would otherwise be given to repeated explanation. This interpretative role of the pastoral counselor can be helpful not only in the initial stages of illness and hospitalization, but it also can be of value in the recuperative and adjustment period as well. The objective yet empathic response to the pastoral counselor to the patient's illness can help lead the patient to a realistic acceptance of his situation.

2. *Support.* In a similar way the pastoral counselor can be of service by giving support to the physician's medical decision. For example, a patient may need the amputation of a limb in order to recover. The patient's reluctance to consent to this surgery is understandable, but it is not in the best interest of his health. As a non-medical person yet concerned, the pastoral counselor is able to reinforce the physician's recommendation as representing an objective and independent viewpoint. Even if the surgery is not radical in scope or emergency in nature, the pastoral counselor's support of the physician's directives can help allay some of the anxiety many patients experience. This "assurance therapy" to the surgical patient extends to the medical patient as well. Also, the pastoral counselor's support of a rehabilitative program may help the patient accept it and apply himself to it more vigorously. Obviously, the impact of the pastoral counselor's supportive role varies from patient to patient, and increases in significance if the patient has no family or other support system performing this function.

Another aspect of the pastoral counselor's supportive function has nothing to do with the patient. This is the support which the pastoral counselor may give to the physician himself. The moral decisions in relation to abortion and prolongation of life, for example, are thrust upon the physician many times. The pastoral counselor's role is not judgmental or may not even be advisory in these instances, but for the physician to know that another individual appreciates and understands his dilemma in such cases can have great supportive value. The pastoral counselor does not duplicate or compete with the physician's own personal pastor, but his availability and sensitivity to the issues involved make him an additional ally.

3. *Liaison.* The pastoral counselor can function as a liaison between the physician and the patient's own minister. This communication link can work several ways. The physician may wish the patient's pastor to cooperate in a program of rehabilitation for a patient needing a prosthesis, for example. The pastoral counselor can contact the pastor so that the physician himself can explain the ways in which the pastor can help, or the pastoral counselor can convey the physician's intent to the pastor. The pastoral counselor is acquainted with other area clergymen and knows where to reach them when needed.

On the other hand, as a liaison the pastoral counselor may bring to the physician's attention some facet of the patient's background that might be relevant to the physician's diagnostic or therapeutic evaluation. For example, the attending physician may be unaware that one of his patients had recently lost a close family member. The pastoral counselor may have prior access to this information and his mentioning this to the physician might permit the physician to view that patient's depression from a different perspective. Treatment procedures and recommendations would be adjusted accordingly.

Similarly, in other instances the pastoral counselor may report to the physician significant aspects of the patient's religious orientation that affect the patient's attitude toward his illness and hospitalization.

4. *Counseling.* Rarely does the physician have the time to spend talking with each of his patients at length. The pastoral counselor can be very useful at this point. The pastoral counselor is specially trained in counseling, but does not attempt any in depth psychotherapy. The presurgery anxiety that is often noted is not in itself indicative of emotional illness or instability and can often be handled effectively by the pastoral counselor. His presence and assurance can help alleviate some of the tension which the patient feels before a surgical procedure. Similarly, his ministry following surgery can help ease post-operative depression.

When the diagnosis is terminal illness, the pastoral counselor may aid the physician by being present when the patient is informed or shortly thereafter. This is never an easy or pleasant task for the physician. The pastoral counselor can help bear this burden and be of help in comforting the patient then and later on with follow-up visits. Again, this service is of special importance when the patient has no regular spiritual advisor or family support system.

Not only does the pastoral counselor minister to the patient, but he can also assist the physician by counseling with the patient's family. Often the patient is heavily sedated and the need in the patient's room is for couseling with the family. This is certainly true immediately after the patient expires. The pastoral counselor is trained to assist the grieving and bereaved.

The pastoral counselor's function in any particular case, of course, should be in coordination and consistent with the physician's professional judgment. Of all the services he may render, the pastoral counselor will always respect the physician's schedule and decisions. Ideally, the pastoral counselor will not "play God" or assume a role for which he is neither qualified or trained. However, his services will be readily rendered for the benefit of the patient and physician alike.

Chapter X

Problem Patients

The population of a hospital is a distorted reflection of the population at large. Distorted because of the effects of illness and hospitalization upon the personality. However, the majority of distortion is quite temporal and minimal. Most hospital patients, like people everywhere, are friendly, kind, and responsive to others. A small minority are "problem" patients. While not discounting the adverse effects of illness referred to above, there remain patients that are so maladjusted that they become difficult for health care personnel to relate to.

Three broad categories of the problem patient will be dealt with herein. The first are those patients who are hostile and abusive to those who are responsible for their care. The second group are problem patients because they employ manipulative behavior not only to achieve their own ends, but engage in it as a manner of relating to society at large. The third category embraces those patients whose behavior becomes a problem because it is self-destructive. These three general classes of patients will be discussed in the order given above.

The Hostile Patient

Everyone wants to be liked. This includes hospital personnel, too. In fact, the desire to be liked for being helpful to others in need has to be one of the strong motivations for being in the health field. This being the case when a hostile patient is encountered, the helper may find him or herself retreating in self-righteous indignation. Consider the following case history:

Frances H., a 55 year old female orthopedic patient had asystematically alienated every nurse and aide on the floor. She sharply criticized her physician, hospital care, diet, etc. Her language and behavior were abusive to staff and unwarranted.

This patient struck out at all the hospital personnel so much so that whenever her light went on, no one wanted to respond. As the nursing staff became adversely emotionally involved, their care deteriorated, creating yet more hostility. Unfortunately, a vicious chain reaction had been put in motion.

This situation is by no means unique in the hospital setting. Patients often express hostility toward their physician, the nursing staff, other hospital personnel and hospital procedure. While a certain amount of hostility can be tolerated, even expected, in many patients, there are times when the sheer magnitude of anger becomes a distinct problem.

In meeting the problem of the hostile patient there are three processes which may be of benefit to explore. These processes can be posed as questions which can be worked through individually or as a group. They will be discussed briefly here.

1. What does this patient do or say that is irritating? This process might be called identification. As feelings and reactions are put into words often a realization of what is abrasive is the first step toward a healthy ventilation. Also, it is easier to communicate frustration to other personnel if it can be verbalized. By identifying and owning feelings, the staff can be brought closer to each other, and this reduces the possibility of manipulation by the patient. Further staff problems can be avoided if thoughts about and emotional reaction to the patient are seen to be general among the hospital staff. This prevents staff from feeling alone or guilty because of their hostile feelings.

Patients' hostility generates a defensive hostility among staff. To defuse the hostility of the personnel, a process of identification can promote a more objective approach to the problem and lessen reactive hostility. A simple listing may be done individually or as a group, orally or in writing. The key is to foster a more analytic examination of the problem which will reduce the incidence of psychological projection and displacement.

2. Why does this patient do or say the things that are irritating? This process is simply one of comprehension. It is the effort made to view things from the perspective of the hostile patient. By focusing attention on what the patient sees as happening, a productive appreciation of the patient's psychological field may emerge.

In the case history used above, it was noted that this particular patient's experience with hospitalization had to be negative. A previous extensive hospital stay had been horrendous because surgery for a total hip replacement had been unsuccessful. Her present situation was not much better since the same surgery on the same hip had resulted in an infection which increased the length of stay considerably. She was almost hysterical with the fear that this second surgery might thus be unsuccessful also and lead to a third surgery she felt she could not afford financially or emotionally.

When the framework of the patient is honestly considered, very often a degree of compassion emerges. This is why comprehension is such an important process. Generally poor communication inhibits the process of comprehension, and the hospital staff reacts in kind. A genuine team approach in which everyone in contact with a hostile patient may contribute a different facet of the patient's situation can be very productive at this point.

3. What constructive and creative response can counteract the hostility of this patient? The third and final process

suggested here is modification. Part of the solution to dealing with this problem patient lay in a change in staff attitude toward the patient's situation and the rest of the solution lay in communicating this changed attitude to the patient.

As the staff considered their feelings about the patient's slow progress, it became evident that the staff had a need to see rapid improvement as much or more as the patient herself. This realization yielded a patience that had somehow been lost during her long hospitalization. As this more relaxed and accepting attitude was translated into direct care and attention, some of the anxiety and fear the patient was experiencing subsided. As the patient's progress rate was accepted for what it was, a more pleasant atmosphere was created and made taking care of her much less obnoxious.

As the patient sensed her care was no longer dreaded by the staff, she became more pleasant and less critical. The unwholesome chain had been reversed and until this patient was discharged her hostility gradually dissipated and disappeared.

The Manipulative Patient

By and large most manipulative patients are in the psychiatric hospitals or in psychiatric wards of general hospitals. However, since mental illness may be seen as a deviation in degree as well as in kind from the population at large, it might be reasonably supposed that patients with definite manipulative tendencies may be encountered occasionally in other hospital areas as well. General hospital staff are often unprepared to cope with this type of problem patient. Consider the following case history:

> Alvin R. a 27 year old male patient was admitted due to a "hunting accident." A gun shot wound in his right foot precipitated amputation just above the ankle. He was extremely polite and pleasant to the staff.

102

This patient's behavior is so patently different from the preceding case history discussed above it might be wondered why he was ever classified as a problem patient. His behavior was exemplary and he soon ingratiated himself to all the hospital staff. Initially, young female nurses were particularly solicitous.

Soon, however, problems became evident. With a slightly different account of his circumstances, he had "borrowed" small sums of money from various staff members. He also had home phone numbers from many of the younger, unmarried nurses. Somehow he had imported enough liquor to get drunk and to bring into the open the fact that he was indeed a problem patient.

It soon became clear that he was using an easy charm and a variety of hard-luck stories to obtain special treatment and privileges. He also was fond of distorting facts to foster bad feeling among the staff toward each other, but never toward himself.

The resolution of his problem behavior was somewhat complicated by his transfer from one unit to another for medical reasons. However, the two processes employed achieved two necessary results. These include communication and confrontation.

1. *Communication.* This process was simply a matter of having everyone in contact with the patient share relevant information about the patient. While hospital personnel are trained to record medical and emotional information, it became necessary to record informally other pertinent patient information as well. The purpose of this was to alert staff members of the patient's attempts to "con" other staff members.

The effect of this procedure was twofold; (1) it made the staff aware of his efforts to use them, and (2) it made the patient realize that he could not play one staff member against another to get special consideration. Once this communication process became operative, the patient's efforts subsided considerably.

2. *Confrontation.* By this is meant that the patient was directly confronted with any inconsistencies in his stories and with firm negatives when he requested extra privileges. This approach also reduced his manipulative behavior. When it became obvious the staff was no longer gullible he began to try to manipulate his roommate's family. This was handled in the same manner and was squelched.

Finally, he gave up trying and made a relatively good adjustment to his hospitalization. He began to do things for himself he was fully capable of doing and accepted more responsibility for his actions. It came out that his "hunting accident" was inflicted by a law enforcement officer, and that he was married even though he had proposed to at least one of the nursing assistants.

Chronic Self-Destructive Behavior

Much needed attention has been given to the study of self-destructive behavior (Schneidman, 1976). Suicide attempts include an almost bizarre variety of methods. Policemen, emergency medical personnel and hospital staff continually see persons who attempt to take their own lives. Obviously, and unfortunately, many of these attempts are successful. Not so obvious, but just as unfortunate, is the fact that many successful attempts are preceeded by unsuccessful attempts.

The overt and covert reasons for opting for suicide are about as varied as are the means elected to commit the act. Apparently the one common thread that runs through each instance is the belief that suicide is the best alternative available. Paradoxically, it would almost seem that suicide is intended to make significant a life devoid of significance. The victim suffers ultimately to call attention to his suffering.

A good deal of emphasis is given to the recognizing of behavioral and personality changes which culminate in a suicide attempt (Miles, 1977). However, the focus here will be on behavior which produces less obvious attempts of self-destruction. These behaviors are nonetheless real and should be of equal concern to health personnel. These less obvious attempts are certainly not as dramatic and are generally more chronic, sustained efforts as opposed sudden, acute action. It is advanced that these attempts are just as much a call for help as more "convention" and overt suicide attempts. Basically, the dynamics are identical - strong masochistic tendencies and low self esteem - or both.

In fact, it would seem that the time factor is the most significant difference between the two groups. Most overt suicide attempts employ overdose of drugs, cut wrists, gunshot wounds, hanging, etc. Alcoholism also may be interpreted as "drug abuse" designed to destroy one's self (Edwards & Grant, 1977). The less obvious attempts to be examined herein are: (1) death by diet; (2) death by neglected treatment; (3) death by deliberate defiance; and (4) death by calculated ignorance. As these are dealt with, it will emerge that the only difference between the obvious and less obvious attempts is degree rather than kind. The goal is identical, and the psychological needs must be almost identical also. Further, the line of difference between "normal" behavior and these attempts would only seem to be drawn by motive.

1. *Death by Diet.* This category of less obvious attempts of self-destruction may be illustrated by the following case history:

> Mrs. Carol C., 49 year old divorced female was a diagnosed diabetic. She knowingly refused to regulate her diet and consequently, developed gangrenous feet, but continued to eat indiscriminately.

By her own admission, she knew the seriousness of her life style and persisted in ignoring medical advice. She said she hoped she would die as she had nothing to live for. Happily, however, she met and married an understanding man. Her desire for life and health returned dramatically and was willingly (if not cheerfully) undergoing painful skin grafting to correct the months of self-abusive behavior. She modified her diet appropriately and was making considerable progress at last contact.

This brief vignette indicates that stress and depression can lead to calculated self-destruction and a gradual nature. As indicated above, many diabetics occasionally indulge in such behavior, thus the abnormality consists in the deliberate persistence of it.

2. *Death by Neglected Treatment.* Consider next, an example of the same principle of a passive yet calculated effort designed for the sole purpose of self-destruction:

> Mrs. Nettie B., 78 year old widow observed the appearance and development of a breast nodule. When, reluctantly, she was seen by a physician, the cancer had metastasized inoperably.

This account could be repeated many times over using different subjects and medical circumstances. In this particular instance the patient verbalized her death wish by stating that she had lost her husband of fifty years, and wanted to be where he was waiting for her.

She was well aware of the consequences of her neglected treatment of a condition that could have been amenable to successful surgery if detected earlier. The results were as certain as if she had held a gun to her head and fired, but the time element was obviously much more prolonged.

3. *Death by Deliberate Defiance.* This third category and accompanying factual anecdote is similar to the first:

Roy N., 70 year old male is a renal dialysis patient. He has been on dialysis for over two years. His fluid intake was limited, but he insisted on drinking two beers every day. Congestive heart failure was listed as cause of death.

In this instance the patient knowingly continued behavior his physician warned against. He, too, verbalized that he was aware of the results of his excessive fluid intake, but would rather die than deprive himself of what he considered an enjoyable element in his life style.

His recognition of what he was inevitably doing to his already strained body system was a continual, deliberate defiance of medical advice. Again, it was only a matter of time and certain eventuality.

4. *Death by Calculated Ignorance*. This final category includes several kinds of behavior. It involves the continual ignoring of risk factors associated with any given illness or health condition. Of many examples that could be used, the following is representative:

Harry B., had a severe myocardial infarction. After his release from the hospital, he resumed smoking two packs of cigarettes daily, stopped a prescribed exercise program, and didn't take prescribed medication. He was brought to the hospital emergency room, DOA, in less than two years.

This actual case history illustrates the point well. While it might be argued that the person involved may be simply rationalizing that such behavior isn't really deleterious to his health, such calculated ignorance of elementary health factors indicates a pathological response.

This is a different type of behavior than that engaged in by most, if not all, persons who occasionally overeat, work too hard, exercise too little, etc. In this instance, the risks are too definite to be consistantly ignored. The certain knowledge of the results of such a life style for a cardiac patient can only be construed as deliberate self-destruction.

These four examples of chronic self-destructive behavior could be duplicated many times over. Health care professionals, depending upon their conscious or subconscious perceptions, will react to specific cases accordingly. If these types of illness/behaviors are determined to be self-destructive, the emotional reaction of the hospital staff, for example, may be as negative as that directed toward patients that engage in overt suicidal behavior. On the other hand, if these types of patients are not consciously perceived as suicidal, the staff may still react negatively and not be aware of the etiology of their feelings. They may see their best efforts wasted on patients that seemingly don't take care of themselves anyway.

The point taken here is that an awareness of the dynamics of chronic self-destructive behavior can significantly affect the attitude of staff to these many patients. Too often the implicit, less dramatic call for help is completely ignored. Behavior often interpreted as unappreciative at best and uncooperative at worst, could better be seen as a plea for attention to the unmet emotional needs of the patients (Groves 1978).

Such an awareness might be demonstrated in the three following ways: (1) Direct patient care should emphasize genuine human concern; (2) Personnel should examine carefully their own feelings about suicidal behavior; (3) Personnel could consider the appropriateness of referral for psychological counseling. These concepts will be briefly discussed below.

1. *Genuine Concern.* Overt suicide is often perceived as an attempt to call attention to oneself, an act of desperation in response to adverse life events (Lancet, 1974). If so, then, the hospital staff as a caring team should be so enlightened that

every effort should be made to demonstrate genuine human concern for the passive suicidal patients. Even though there are indications that the actual suicide rate is higher among persons who make a "serious" suicide attempt than those whose overt attempts are considered "less serious" (Rosen, 1976); a caring response is still certainly in order for those patients who engage in less obvious self-destructive behavior.

2. *Staff Emotions.* As staff awareness emerges and perceives less obvious attempts at self-destruction for what they are, there must be an accompanying awareness of personal feelings. All health care professionals are dedicated to the preserving and extending of life. There persists a certain revulsion toward suicide patients, since that for which health professionals fight—life—is being willingly surrendered. Inner contradictions may be experienced by staff who work primarily with acute, overt suicidal patients. In the same way staff recognition of their feelings, the so-called "gut reaction", toward the passive suicidal patient needs to be honestly explored and resolved. This is necessary for maximum patient care as well as high staff morale, which are difficult to separate (Groves, 1978).

3. *Referral.* Many studies of self-inflicted injury and self-mutilation indicate the prevalence of psychiatric disturbance with these patients (Sneddon & Sneddon, 1975; Herzberg, 1977). In a sense overt suicide patients present more a psychiatric than a physical profile. To deal only with the physical is to do great injustice to the needs of the patient as a total person. Similarly, hospital staff need to be cognizant of the need for psychological counseling for the passive self-destructive patient as well. Very possibly the physical prognosis will be inextricably bound to the attitude changes the patient makes as well as his medical management.

A person is only as strong as the weaknesses he acknowledged. To make a psychological referral is not a "cop-out" or indication of inability to handle this type of patient, but is rather a recognition that no one person in the hospital can be all things to all patients at all times.

Summary

Patients may deliberately engage in behavior (commission or ommission) which is detrimental to their health. It is advanced that these patients are indulging in chronic self-destructive activity, little different from the more dramatic acute suicide attempt. By neglecting, ignoring, and defying medical advice and knowledge, that patient eventually accomplishes his purpose without the guilt and stigma of suicide. The patient's life style is geared toward what has been referred to as "partial death." (Menninger, 1938)

As health care personnel recognize this type of patient and their own feelings, hopefully this behavior can be modified and even extinguished. Sometimes this involves psychiatric referral for extreme cases when genuine human caring seems too little or too late. Hopefully by listening to these patients' call for help, their needs as whole human beings can be met.

SECTION THREE

Specific Counseling Situations

Chapter XI
Counseling

Parents of
Stillborn Babies

Rapid advances in medical technology have resulted in a decreasing rate of infant mortality. Unfortunately, infants still do die both at the hospital and at home. Recently, a good deal has been written about S.I.D.S. (Sudden Infant Death Syndrome). In these cases of "crib death" the newborn has often been alive for a period of days, weeks or even months. However, the focus of this chapter will be on the stillborn infant whose death precedes or is simultaneous with its birth. The psychological impact stillbirth has on the parents is somewhat different than other types of infant death. More often the pastoral counselor is in a direct relation to the bereaved mother for a period of at least several days while she is hospitalized. Thus, he is in a position to give a great deal of help and support to the mother during this time.

Even nurses who have spent a number of years on the obstetric unit often feel awkward and uncomfortable about relating to this kind of patient. Nurses who seek assignment to this area of work feel a sense of defeat and frustration when their best efforts do not result in a live birth. In order to be of help to the patient and the nurse, the pastoral counselor must work through his own feelings about what has happened. Then, the pastoral counselor will have to relate to a patient who is very sensitive about how he acts and about what he says or does not say.

A natural reaction on the part of the pastoral counselor may be to attempt to comfort the mother by using cliches. He should not tell her that her baby is "better off where he is." As Eason (1970) points out, the parents of a baby view the baby as an extension of themselves. By a not very subtle process of identification, the parents see a part of themselves in the baby and nobody likes to be told that a part of them is better off dead than living.

According to Schoenberg, et al (1970), the loss of a child is the most devastating experience a family can have. In view of this, an emotionality that is considerably heightened can be anticipated. Each stage of the grieving process will be accentuated and intensified. Even though the life of the stillborn infant is so extremely brief in a social sense, the mother has already been living with that life for the previous nine months. Her emotional attachment has been strong for months before delivery was expected.

At this point, it is productive to examine the special grief process of the mother and relate it to the five grief stages as outlined by Kubler-Ross (1969). These stages are, of course, not always in a specific order or experienced by every mother every time, but they do offer a general framework of which to be aware.

1. *Denial.* Often the first stage in the grieving process is a denial of the infant's death. In some cases, even though the physician cannot detect a heartbeat before labor, the mother is convinced that her baby is not really dead. Similarly, when informed after delivery that her baby is not alive, the mother may fantasize and even verbalize the conviction that the dead baby is not her own. In some instances she may even persist in a belief that the dead baby is not her own, but that it is a case of mistaken identity.

Whatever form it takes, denial is generally encountered in most instances. It has been suggested that the amount of

114

shock and disbelief a mother experiences is in proportion to the amount of medication given to her (Zahourek & Jensen, 1973). The denial is not limited to only the mother, but it is experienced by other family members as well (Bird, 1973).

Employed as a defense mechanism, denial serves to postpone the acceptance of the reality of death. It is useful to the extent that it allows a certain amount of time before grief must be faced. It becomes harmful and pathological when it blocks out and prevents the grieving process altogether.

At this point, the pastoral counselor is confronted with the necessity of responding in some fashion to expressions of denial. He must be gentle, yet firm. He must never contribute to the patient's fantasy, but always be empathic and understanding. A simple, honest statement might be helpful, such as, "Yes, it is your baby, but I'm very sorry. I know it must hurt."

A difference of hospital policy is noted with regard to letting the mother see the stillborn baby. Those who advocate this procedure contend that it dispels denial and enables the mother to begin working through her grief. Further, it is argued that it prevents unwholesome speculation concerning her baby's normal development. On the other hand, those who oppose letting the mother see her baby do so on the grounds that the emotional shock of losing the baby is too much already for the mother and that viewing the baby only upsets the mother more.

Whether the mother's seeing her baby is or is not a therapeutic experience depends upon adequate preparation of the mother beforehand. The nurse's own reaction to the appearance of the stillborn baby will be a big factor in how the mother will react. In any event, the parents' wishes should be considered (Seitz and Warrick, 1974).

2. *Anger.* A second stage of the normal grief process is anger. Instead of "Not me!" it is "Why me?" The mother of

the stillborn infant may well ponder "Why mine?" Especially if the mother prides herself on taking good care of her children, she will be angry and indignant that her baby is not alive for her to take care of. This anger is a product of her feelings of loss, loneliness and being cheated. As Eason (1970) notes: "During the normal process of mourning, the grieving family members feel anger and irritation at the loss they are experiencing. They are losing a relationship that has been meaningful to them. . ."

As is true in much venting of anger, it is focused on persons and objects near at hand, regardless of their objective connection to the source of the anger. Thus anger, is frequently vented on the physician, hospital staff, etc. There is a basic feeling of powerlessness and helplessness which cannot be rationally attacked (Hagan, 1974). Death is a very abstract and elusive enemy, but the pastoral counselor is quite concrete and visible, and may come in for his share of vented anger.

The natural tendency of the pastoral counselor is to respond defensively. This is done not only by becoming angry at the mother, but by avoiding her as much as possible as well. The mother herself may not be aware of the dynamics which make her strike out against others, but the pastoral counselor should be cognizant of his own feelings toward the patient. Ideally, the pastoral counselor should help the angered, bereaved mother to re-channel her psychic energy used in anger into constructive combat. This can be done by enlisting the mother in fighting against the disease that may have been responsible for the stillbirth, by encouraging the mother to fight for better research facilities and programs.

In this regard perhaps an appropriate response might be: "We here at the hospital are angry, too, that a life is gone. Perhaps when you get home, you can help some of the organizations that are trying to eliminate the causes of stillbirth." By re-directing the mother's energy, it makes anger socially acceptable and relieves the feelings of guilt which often accompany socially unacceptable behavior.

Another issue to be considered at this point is whether the mother who lost her baby should remain on the maternity floor or be transferred to another unit within the hospital. As the bereaved mother sees mothers and their live, healthy babies, she may well be forced to ponder why others are living and hers is dead. Generally speaking, the mother may emotionally fare better on a different floor or unit where she is not constantly reminded of babies' feeding times, etc. If this is not possible, the mother should at least have a private room. Again, the pastoral counselor can be of assistance in helping the bereaved mother working through this stage by tactfully pointing out that the living babies and their mothers were in no way responsible for her baby's death.

3. *Bargaining.* A third stage of grief involves bargaining. This procedure is probably omitted in the case of the death of the stillborn, especially if it is sudden and unexpected. If, however, the baby dies postpartum (after birth) and not antepartum or intrapartum (before or during birth), there may be a brief period in which the mother who is aware that things are not well with her baby may bargain. Further, bargaining may have been going on for the past months if the mother was worried that her baby would not be born alive and "normal."

Subconsciously or consciously, she may bargain that if her baby is alive and well, she will dedicate it to God or the church. Or she may promise herself that she will try to be a better wife and mother or person in any dimension. The emotional danger with bargaining is the instance of stillbirth. The mother may feel that God or "fate" has dealt her a cruel blow. She is at a loss to explain what went wrong. In searching for a cause, she may easily slip into feelings of guilt and depression.

117

4. *Depression.* This fourth stage seems to be fairly universal in the grief process. The pastoral counselor encounters this when he enters the room of the bereaved mother and finds her weeping or staring dejectedly out the window. Clinically, she appears to be preoccupied and is slow to respond to simple directions. The degree of withdrawal indicates the depth of the depression. Conceivably, it may become so profound as to indicate psychiatric referral.

Studies indicate that even after a year's duration mothers who have lost a newborn evince a significant depression when compared to a control group (Jensen and Sahourek, 1972). This depression is closely tied to feelings of guilt and blame. The following verbatim illustrates this relationship: ". . . if only I could be sure I didn't do anything to make her die. I had the German measles, and I worried so. But the doctor said her not being able to breathe rightly didn't come from the measles" (Russell, 1975).

The pastoral counselor is also in a critical position to give accurate medical information to the mother to combat false guilt and blame. Even the well-educated, enlightened mother may have a repertoire of medical superstition which needs to be dispelled. The pastoral counselor may want to initiate a conversation with the prelude, "Many mothers feel that they are somehow responsible for the baby's death . . ." This opens the door for comments and questions which the mother might be reluctant to discuss with her physician or family. An open and accepting attitude and a frank, professional reply may save the mother a lot of "hang-ups" regarding her role in the death of the baby.

Compounding the natural depression which is a part of psychological grief is the physiological post-partum depression. These phenomenon affects 60 to 100 percent of all mothers and usually appears 24 to 48 hours after delivery (Rovinsky and Guttmacher, 1965). Post-partum depression is similar to that depression which follows the loss of any part of the body. However, it seems to be more pronounced and of longer duration in mothers of the stillborn. Certainly this compounded depression cannot be dealt with during the hospital stay. As Hagan (1974) points out: "Parents need to be told that they will not always feel this way; that the grieving process takes time, and only time will make the difference."

5. *Acceptance.* As indicated above, the grief process will not end with the hospital stay. The final stage of acceptance may not be seen by the pastoral counselor at all. Hopefully, the seeds of acceptance will have been sown and nurtured by all the hospital staff. The degree of acceptance the bereaved mother achieves is a product of many individual difference. The mother's age, cultural heritage, religious tradition, number of living children before and after the stillbirth, will all influence the mother's (and family's) acceptance of the baby's death. This is to say nothing of those complex psychological variables that influence personal adjustment also.

The way in which the mother behaves subsequently is a clue to the adjustment she has made. Depending upon the factors listed above, she may resolve her grief by deciding to get pregnant immediately and have a baby to "take the place" of the stillborn. Or, she may definitely decide never to become pregnant again. A third possibility is to decide to "wait and see," i.e., she does not have the responsibility of making a choice of either alternative.

In any event, the mother may later consult with the physician and the pastoral counselor and try to have them make the decision for her. The pastoral counselor must be sure to let any resolve be that which is genuinely the mother's own. The giving of pertinent information is the physician's role, and the pastoral counselor must be careful not to adopt the role of decision maker.

The greatest help the pastoral counselor can be is to give a warm and accepting atmosphere in which as much healing as possible can take place. This means not being uncomfortable when the mother needs to cry and being with her or giving her privacy as her mood indicates.

Even though the contact of the pastoral counselor will be primarily with the mother, it should be noted that his contact with the father is important also. This is true because the mother of the stillborn emotionally interacts with her husband more than anyone else. The quality of their relationship will be a factor in how well the mother can handle the normal grief process.

As Gilson (1976) points out, grieving is a process undergone by all family members who are directly affected by a death. Therefore, the husband will presumably go through the same stages as his wife. However, the rate and order of those stages will probably be somewhat different. He will have a different immediate environment not being hospitalized and there will not be physiological concomitants to deal with. Thus his progress may well be more rapid and he may come to acceptance sooner. He may even find it difficult to be patient with his wife as she moves at a slower rate.

Here again, the pastoral counselor can be therapeutic. By being cognizant of the differences in working through the grief process he can help the husband understand his wife's slower or different progress. The pastoral counselor can also understand how her husband's visits might upset his wife. By helping the husband understand his wife's emotional and physical circumstances the pastoral counselor can help the husband assist rather than impede his wife's progress. The pastoral counselor's role here should not be underestimated.

The pastoral counselor may want to make it a point to talk with the husband before or after his visit to help interpret his wife's emotional behavior and his own feelings. He can enlist his aid and cooperation in the total treatment program. Depending upon their proximity and depth of relationship, the parents, in-laws and other children may need help and support from the pastoral counselor as they interact with the mother of the stillborn and go through the grief process also.

In summary, the pastoral counselor's response both verbal and non-verbal can be immensely helpful and supportive of the mother of the stillborn. By empathic understanding of the various stages of the grieving process, the pastoral counselor is in a position to be a therapeutic agent emotionally as well as physically. This attention to the psychological needs of the patient contributes greatly to the treating of the whole person.

Chapter XII

Counseling the Surgical Patient

The uniqueness of the individual is no more apparent than in his reaction to the stress of surgery. Not only are there physical and anatomical differences which make each surgical procedure unique, but there are also psychological reactions to surgery which are idiosyncratic. Notwithstanding the individual differences involved, the effects of presurgical anxiety are uniformly against the best interest of the patient. Perhaps at no other point do mind and body interact in such obvious and deleterious fashion.

As Ramsay (1972 points out:

> *Emotional and environmental stresses may also have a direct effect on the metabolism of cardiac muscle which leads to degenerative processes that are not related to coronary closure as such. Myocardial damage may result from hypoxia and electrolyte derangements due to hormonal changes resulting from emotion.*

This same evaluation is advanced by Williams, et al (1969) who contend:

> *Excessive preoperative anxiety appears to affect a patient's physiological status markedly at the time of operation.*

So for these reasons, an examination of how to minister to the pre-surgical patient seems warranted.

The organization of this chapter will consist of four basic divisions: (1) The Etiology of Pre-Surgical Anxiety, (2) Relevant Research, (3) A Possible Model, and (4) The Pastoral Counselor's Role.

I. The Etiology of Pre-Surgical Anxiety

As with most behavioral phenomena, the etiology of pre-surgical anxiety is not directly attributable to a single factor operating independently of all others. It is not possible to isolate any one variable which is always present in every patient. However, a number of variables can be examined which seem to be logically interrelated. Also, it is a reasonable assumption that the stress of surgery will not be greatly unlike the stress discerned in other stress producing situations. As Janis (1958) puts it:

> *From a psychological standpoint, a major surgical operation constitutes a stress situation which resembles many other types of catastrophes and disasters in that the 'victim' faces a combination of three major forms of imminent danger—the possibility of suffering acute pain, of undergoing serious body damage, and of dying.*

This being the case, the main causes of stress, per se, can be suspected as playing a role in pre-surgical anxiety. Moreover, the extent to which environment may contribute to stress, the unique environmental milieu of the hospital can be viewed as a contributory cause. Therefore, a hospital patient has to deal with two aspects of anxiety: (1) those factors which arise from within the individual, and (2) those factors which arise from without and aggravate the inner stress.

Admittedly it is difficult to differentiate between the endogenous and exogenous factors which are involved in the etiology of pre-surgical anxiety. The discussion is divided in this way for organizational purposes only and no sharp line of demarcation is usually discernable at the clinical level.

124

1. *Fear of the Unknown.* One thesis often advanced is that the etiology of pre-surgical anxiety is rooted in the fear of the unknown; therfore, the alleviation of the symptoms will be seen in proportion to the information and support given. Johnson (1967) says:

> *Patients always experience a certain amount of apprehension before surgery, even when the operation is a minor one. Basically, this is an expression of fear of the unknown which may be exaggerated by fear of the anesthetic, the actual operation or its outcome.*

Even though a patient has experienced a relatively recent hospitalization, there is no guarantee that a present surgery is greeted calmly. Graham and Conley (1971) using empirical methodology examined this variable and concluded:

> *There was no significant difference ($x_2 = .010$), therefore, previous hospitalization cannot be said to be associated with either low or higher levels of anxiety.*

However, a past surgery (not hospitalization) may itself be a complicating force in handling the present anxiety. This is because the patient usually conceives of his present and future circumstances to be more threatening than the past. Thus, the temporal proximity of present minor surgery can create more anxiety than the memory of a successful major surgery can allay. Further, this is particularly true if the anxiety of the previous surgery was not dealt with adequately. The suppressed anxiety may surface again as a subconscious "flashback." It follows then that although a patient has experienced a successful surgery, his present needs should not be discounted or ignored.

2. *Fear of Outcome.* Especially when the surgical procedure is exploratory in nature, the fear of what might be discovered contributes to the patient's anxiety. Even in a so-called routine operation the fear of what might be encountered is a strong negative force. In our society, the dread of

cancer is very real and present, the visions of malignancy dance before the imagination of many surgical patients. For example, Ramsay (1972) found that 100% of the patients undergoing breast lump surgery are afraid of cancer.

For those who undergo surgery, knowing a previous biopsy indicates a malignancy, there is also the fear that it might be impossible to remove the cancerous tissue or organ completely, or that it is in an advanced stage and spread throughout the body. Even with the physicians' assurances to the contrary, some patients will maintain their high anxiety level, believing at the "gut level" that their doctor is deliberately misleading them.

3. *Fear of Death*. For many patients, the fear of death has a spiritual as well as a physical dimension. For in some persons death *per se* is not as feared as is the hereafter. Often one's religious beliefs include an uncertainty about the attainment of eternal bliss. There is held out the possibility of dying under the judgment and wrath of God; and inasmuch as the surgery may not be successful, the surgery becomes the agency or means by which one enters eternity. As the time of surgery approaches, the anxiety heightens if the patient entertains uncertainty about his relationship to God. The punitive and judgmental aspects of religious teaching are interpreted in an unconstructive way until the patient may be almost immobilized with fear, and hesitate to consent to the surgery.

On the other hand, a patient whose religious faith is working for him can derive great inner strength which is a great asset in the surgical procedure. Bruegel (1972), using a sample of eighty-five surgical patients, gave them the IPAT Anxiety Scale the evening before surgery. Independent variables she included were age, sex, socio-economic status, education, religion, race, type of surgery, etc. The dependent variable was the number of analgesic medications, requested the first forty-eight hours post-operatively. She found:

126

The relationship between anxiety and religion was the only one with significance: persons with no stated religious preference were much more anxious than either Protestants or Catholics (F = 3.17, p .05).

4. *Dependency Needs.* Another factor besides fear of the unknown, which is believed to be involved in the etiology of pre-surgical anxiety, is what may be referred to as dependency needs. According to this line of thought, most people can be classified with respect to behavior which is labelled high or low dependency. Further, the extremes on the dependency continuum are to be avoided. Thus, those patients who find it difficult to allow themselves to be dependent on anyone (low dependency) find it difficult to adopt a role of dependency such as hospitalization and surgery require. As Williams (1973) notes:

If such a person is forced into a dependent role through illness . . . he will experience a great anxiety and threat to self-esteem.

By the same token, patients who rate high on a dependency scale and are very dependent experience great anxiety also. As Williams (1973) further remarks:

Illness and hospitalization can be extremely traumatic for such a person in that his psychological dependency, already excessively great, becomes completely blown out of proportion with the actual need to be physically cared for while ill.

5. *Type of Control.* Closely related to the dependency factor in producing pre-surgical anxiety is the type of control to which an individual feels subjected. Some individuals feel that the control of events which influence them are entirely out of their hands. Fate, the will of God, etc., exercise final control over their lives. These persons believe in external control. On the other hand, others feel that what happens to them is dependent on their own behavior. They believe that

127

they "call the shots" and are responsible for their own destiny; they adhere to a belief in internal control.

Research which examines the relationship of this internal/external control variable on preoperative fear and postoperative recovery indicates that the length of postoperative stay is influenced by internal/external control and birth order. Johnson, et al (1970) found:

> The data showed that first borns stayed longer the higher their scores on internal control.

The addition to these endogenous factors (within the patients) are the exogenous factors (outside the patient). The hospital, as the locus of the surgery, introduces a unique set of environmental stimuli which impinge upon the patient's perceptual field.

Although no suggestion is made that the factors discussed here are the only ones involved, they do seem to operate in the creation and maintenance of pre-surgical anxiety. Several exogenous factors will be suggested, but no significance is intimated by their order of presentation. Again, it is emphasized that all of the elements indicated here may or may not be present in any one patient but probably at least one is in evidence in most cases.

6. *Visual Perspective.* Depending upon the degree of consciousness the patient has, his visual position may contribute to the aggravation of his anxiety. Normally, the patient's visual field is perceived from a standing or vertical position. Except perhaps in the case of the chronically ill or bedfast patient, the surgical patient is placed in a horizontal position, often suddenly. His journey to the operating room is perceived from an entirely different perspective. Further, the movement of the cart, the loss of modesty involved in "prepping" procedures, and the effect of the sedative administered may make the patient feel uneasy and threatened.

128

Feeling vulnerable, the patient may demonstrate the pre-surgical anxiety syndrome.

7. *Loss of Consciousness.* Unless the surgery can be performed utilizing a local anesthetic the patient will be given a general anesthetic involving loss of consciousness. For some patients, the fear of being "put under" is greater than the fear of the surgical procedure itself. At times, this fear can be verbalized and brought out into the open and owned. In other cases, it is submerged to a lower level of consciousness and can contribute to the general anxiety the patient experiences. It is possible that the fear of the loss of consciousness if closely aligned with the fear of death and the two fears become confused and intertwined.

In a study reported by Ramsay (1972) 382 patients (182 male, 199 female) were interviewed twenty-four hours before surgery. According to a clinical assessment of anxiety, 73% of the patients had pre-operative fears and 62% of these indicated that the anesthetic was their primary fear.

8. *Pre-Surgical Preparation.* It is ironic that the fear of surgery may be increased by the very necessity of preparation for surgery. Because of the obvious need for sterility, various "prepping" procedures are carried out prior to surgery. The patient often is aware that something beyond ordinary hospital routine is occurring. It is possible that the patient may misinterpret the intentness and efficiency with which the nurse carries out these duties and may become frightened. Especially is this true when part of the procedure involves receiving an injection or limiting the patient's physical movements in any way. His wearing of the surgical attire may make some patients feel self-conscious and ill at ease.

9. *Prevailing Myths.* Possibly each surgical patient has his own personal repertoire of myths concerning surgery in general. This repertoire consists of a combination of the patient's own experience of surgery or that of a close family

129

member or friend, plus an accumulation of debris from popular magazines and TV shows. Misconceptions and distortions may create a milieu in which the patient is steeped in old wives' tales. In pregnancy and childbirth, for example, these myths may be more highly verbalized and obvious than surgery. However, each patient likely maintains a highly personalized store of attitudes and emotions concerning surgery, most of which are anxiety-producing.

The patient's family may compound his anxiety by hovering over him before surgery, uttering false assurances and inane cliches. These well-meaning gestures may be the trigger which sets off a whole barrage of unwholesome sentimentality.

II. Relevant Research on Pre-Surgical Anxiety

1. *Assessment.* In addition to a consideration of the etiology of pre-surgical anxiety, a brief examination of the literature is indicated. Much of the empirical research conducted with hospital in-patients as subjects deals with the assessment of the anxiety the patient experiences. The reason for this emphasis is obvious, for no experimental data can be tested for significance unless and until a valid and reliable dependent variable is found. In order to assess accurately the effect of emotional and environmental variables, an accurate means of measuring anxiety is mandatory.

Several investigators have tackled this problem, each using different approaches. Some have used the existing psychological tests to measure the amount of anxiety encountered prior to surgery. For example, those using Cattell and Schiere's Anxiety Scale Questionnaire include Williams, *et al* (1969) and Bruegel (1971). Others, such as Wolfer and Davis (1970), use observer ratings and self-reporting scales and inventories. Still others devised an adjective check list as did Johnson, *et al* (1970); Graham, *et al* (1971) used a printed guide composed of twenty-four characteristics. Winslow and

Fuhs (1973) also developed a check list form to show baseline pre-operative information; Shetler (1972) developed her own "Operating Room Pre-Operative Interview Sheet" for use by the operating room nurse.

In addition to using printed or published measures, some studies rely on the clinical face to face interview. Among those utilizing this technique are Graham and Conley (1971) and Ramsay (1972). Graham's study concluded: "The most useful and frequently occurring indicators of pre-operative anxiety were the subjective responses of the patients during both the pre-operative period and post-operative visit" (1971, p. 121).

A physiological approach to the measurement of pre-surgical anxiety was made by Williams, *et al* (1969). Their instrument is called the Skin Conductance Anxiety Test (SCAT) which they feel has unique value in providing a reliable, valid and quantitative index of patient anxiety. The technique involves the administration of a 2 cc/min. infusion of a general anesthetic (2.5% thiopental sodium) to reduce and stabilize the galvanic skin response (GSR). The quantity of the drug needed to accomplish this gives the measure of pre-surgical anxiety. Thus, the more drug necessary to eliminate the spontaneous GSR, the higher the level of patient anxiety.

2. *Individual Differences.* Several facets of individual differences have been the object of various studies. For instance, Ramsay (1972) concluded that age was a factor in the amount of pre-surgical anxiety which a patient experiences. He found that patients at both ends of the age scale have less fear; that is, children and patients over sixty. Included in this study was the finding that sex differences are slight—70% of the male and 76% of the females showed anxiety according to clinical assessment. Graham and Conley (1971) also found females to be slightly more anxious than men; but found no statistically significant differences in age. However, no pa-

tients below the age of twenty were included in their sampling. Wolfer and Davis (1970) also found that female patients reported more fear than male patients.

Using a sample of 85 surgical patients (age range: 18 to 70 years) and the number of post-operative analgesic medication needed, Bruegel (1971) examined age, sex, social-economic status, education, religion, race and type of surgery. She found no significant differences except with respect to religion, as noted above.

III. A Possible Model of Pre-Surgical Anxiety

Another perspective on pre-surgical anxiety can be obtained by viewing the surgical procedure in terms of classical approach-avoidance conflict. It is herein advanced that some, probably not all, anxiety preceding surgery can be explained in these terms. Three brief case studies will be included to illustrate the possible application of these hypothetical constructs.

> (1) John S., twenty-six year old male patient is admitted as an in-patient via the emergency room with a diagnosis of possible appendicitis. He has never been in a hospital as a patient before and has been in apparently excellent health. His abdominal pain is severe with nausea. Upon obtaining a lab report, the physician informs John that an immediate appendectomy is necessary.

What level of anxiety will be expected before surgery? Probably low. This is anticipated in that the patient faces a relatively simple approach-avoidance conflict. The positive valence of pain reduction is greater than the negative valence of the surgery to be performed. This situation can be viewed from the perspective of the hedonist—we avoid what causes pain and seek the gratification of comfort needs. Surgery is perceived as that which will give relief and so it produces no great amount of anxiety. No doubt this is an oversimplica-

132

tion since many other variables may enter the picture. For example, the patient may have lost a near relative who had an appendectomy, etc. Generally, however, the basic expectation is for a low level of pre-surgical anxiety.

Consider another case:

(2) Hazel J., thirty-one year old mother of two small children has been in the hospital several days. The lab report on a breast nodule biopsy defintely confirmed a malignancy. The patient is informed by the physician of the finding and of the need for a radical mastectomy.

What level of anxiety will be encountered before surgery? Probably high. This is anticipated in that the patient faces an avoidance-avoidance conflict. The fear of the pain of surgery and the threat to her female body-image is a powerful negative valence, but a negative valence is also present if surgery is not performed in that the malignancy would develop unchecked. Facing two undesirable alternatives characteristically will produce vacillation, tension and a high level of pre-surgical anxiety. The patient probably will verbalize concern for her husband's and children's welfare.

Consider yet a third instance:

(3) Austin H., is an eighty-five year old widower in the intensive care unit. His diagnosis is lower GI bleeding. The X-ray report shows a large tumor in the colon. Surgery is indicated and the patient is informed of this.

What level of anxiety will he manifest prior to surgery? Probably low. In this case the negative valence of fear of death due to surgery is minimized and the positive valence of fear of death due to surgery is minimized and the positive valence of the improvement of body function is maximized, making for little indecision, less vacillation and anxiety. The patient verbalizes willingness and readiness to die.

These three cases are examples of possible formulation for predicting the level of pre-surgical anxiety. Most simply put, to use this model only three questions need be determined:

(1) What positive aspects of the surgical procedure are perceived by the patient?

(2) What negative aspects of the surgical procedure are perceived by the patient?

(3) Which valence dominates?

In determining negative valence, it should be noted that for most patients, regardless of the scope of the surgery, surgery itself is a traumatic experience. Holst and Kurtz (1973) made the observation that there is no such thing as "minor surgery" to the patient. Bouchard and Owens (1972) note:

> Every person will respond to this information (necessity of surgery) according to his own conception of what such surgery means. This will include (1) the physical, psychological, social and financial sacrifices and discomforts involved and (2) anticipation of the outcome of the surgery—whether his condition will be improved or whether he will have a greater disability as a result of the surgery. Because of the threat that impending surgery represents to him, the patient may become withdrawn, exhibit signs of denial, "put up a brave front," or act positively.

Butler and Lewis (1973) further state:

> People tend to become upset about any subtractive surgery, especially if it is a major subtraction like hysterectomy.

These negative aspects contribute greatly to the building up of the patient's anxiety to a crescendo. Often the positive aspects of a surgery are small or non-existent. For these

134

reasons, the pastoral counselor needs to understand and emphathize with the surgical patient. His role in helping will be considered next.

IV. The Pastoral Counselor's Role

Whatever model one considers there are many factors which are involved in any given instance of pre-surgical anxiety. However, the recognition and acknowledgement of the contributory agents and situations examined herein may give some clues to the reduction of such anxiety. The pastoral counselor is apt to encounter many pre-surgical patients in his schedule in various levels of anxiety. Generally speaking, the level of anxiety will increase as the time of surgery draws nearer.

Some patients have been scheduled for surgery weeks or months in advance; for others, surgery is a sudden emergency decision. Depending upon the individual, it seems that the patient who is suddenly aware of the necessity of surgery is able to verbalize his fears more easily than the one who has known for sometime that surgery was planned; however, his level of anxiety may actually be higher. Perhaps this is because the fears are nearer to the surface of con- sciousness and there is no time to indulge in the usual submersive processes.

In any event, the pastoral counselor can be of great assistance to the patient, his family and the surgical team. While he attempts no in-depth psychotherapy, he does listen acceptingly and helps the patient to verbalize and to own his fears. Often, the patient only wants opportunity to acknow- ledge his fears to another, caring human being. As Johnson (1967) puts it:

> *It is important that the pre-operative patient feels free to express his fears . . . for fear always seems to diminish once it is brought into the open.*

135

Characteristically, the patient's family will not listen to or empathize with the patient's fears but will try to deny them or to minimize the unpleasant realities of the situation.

It is important that the pastoral counselor explore the depths of the patient's despair and anxiety fully. The patient does not want or need a superficial, pollyannish glossing over of his feelings. The pastoral counselor should strive to create an atmosphere or acceptance and understanding of the patient's attitude. Even if it seems that the patient's fears are disproportionate to his circumstances, the pastoral counselor should not minimize those fears. They are very real to the patient. On the other hand, if the pastoral counselor has reason to believe that the patient does not react appropriately to the seriousness of the surgery, he should open the door to as full a discussion of the surgery as is productive. Often the patient's denial is the best defense mechanism he can construct.

The pastoral counselor, however, not only listens attentively but communicates to the patient God's abiding love and continuing concern for all His creation. By using selected Scripture passages that emphasize the eternal good purposes of God, the pastoral counselor can help by assuring the patient that God never fails or forsakes but is as near as he will permit Him to be. In his prayers, he emphasizes and underlines the sincere concern for one human being for another in a time of uncertainty and invokes the blessing of the transcendent God who formed man in His own image.

Another significant aspect of ministering to the pre-surgical patient is the administration of the sacraments. The desire for the sacraments will largely reflect the patient's theological orientation; however, the pastoral counselor should be alert to emphasize his willingness to assist in the patient's desire.

A pastoral counselor's visit is also indicated for those

136

patients who have been scheduled for surgery, and their surgery is suddenly cancelled. Whether it is cancelled due to a change in the patient, such as an elevated temperature or electrolyte imbalance, or because of a change in the scheduling the result may be the same. This type of pre-surgical patient may be either depressed or hostile or both.

While the pastoral counselor will never attempt to "play doctor," he can offer routine explanations and give general information, especially to one facing surgery for the first time. At the same time, he stands ready to convey to the patient any aspect of the surgical procedure which the physician may direct. This holds true particularly following surgery and may include the family as well as the patient.

In summary, as the pastoral counselor recognizes the various sources of pre-surgical anxiety he is in a better position to help the patient, his family and the hospital staff by identifying himself with the needs of the patient and interpreting to the patient some of the reasons for his pre-surgical anxiety. Again, the importance of his praying with the patient before surgery cannot be overemphasized. To assure the patient of the availability of God's healing grace is of tremendous value in overcoming the negative effects of pre-surgical anxiety.

Chapter XIII

Counseling with
the Cardiac Patient

Any illness which requires hospitalization poses a threat to the ego integrity of the individual. The defense mechanisms of the psyche begin to operate upon (and sometimes even before) admission. Experienced hospital personnel recognize the various outward manifestations of anxiety such as hostility, withdrawal, etc. This chapter will concentrate upon the personality changes which characterize the cardiac patient. A good deal has been written about the personality variables which may predispose an individual to have heart disease (See Friedman and Roseman, 1974), but the emphasis here will be on those personality variable which come into play following an initial attack. As Wrzesniewski (1975) notes:

> Attitudes toward both the illness and the situation
> produced by treatment and rehabilitation play an
> essential role in the early stages of treatment, as well as
> later when the patient resumes his vocational and social
> life.

Admittedly, any change in effect will vary from patient to patient, but the unique mystique of a myocardial infarction is such that the changes are perhaps more predictable than other illnesses (Cassem and Hackett, 1971). In addition to variations due to individual differences, there will obviously be variations in degree due to the severity of the attack and the attending prognosis. The focus of this paper will be on the male patient, forty to sixty years of age, who has suffered his first mild to moderate heart attack, or myocardial infarction. It is suggested by this writer that the behavior of such patients will include one or more of the characteristic reactions. These are: (1) Denial Reaction, (2) Phobic Reaction, (3) Guilt Reaction, and (4) Depression. These reactions and the pastoral counselor's response to these reactions will be discussed in the order given above.

I. Denial Reaction

A typical reaction, at least initially, for most of the cardiac patients is that of denial. The patient may verbalize his belief that the diagnosis is incorrect. He will attribute his pain to "indigestion" and will feel that the precautions and procedures in the CCU are unnecessary. This patient may be difficult for the physician and nurse to manage and may resist efforts to restrict his activities. Psychologically, it is easier and less threatening to deny the reality of his condition than to admit to his own finitude and vulnerability. For to accept the concept of vulnerability and his own mortality would breed a host of conflicts and questions he is not yet ready to face.

Even verbally the patient may indicate his denial by referring to his condition euphemistically as a "spell," "upset," etc. He will hesitate to use the word "heart" at all (Foster and Andreoli, 1970). This type of patient will hinder efforts of the nurisng staff to do anything for him and thus presents a nursing care problem as well. In extreme cases, he may reject oxygen, refuse to remain bedfast, balk at taking needed medication, etc. This type of behavior is not limited to the hospital environment, but it is exhibited at home as well. Thus the patient will disregard limitations on his activities and will attempt to engage in activities against his own best interests. Even when his own family attempts to remind him of his "condition" he may become belligerent and abusive to them (Tyzenhouse, 1973).

140

All this behavior seems to stem from the patient's not accepting the reality of the myocardial infarction. It is as if he denies it, it will not be real. As with any defense mechanism, the symptoms will persist as long as the person perceives the situation as being threatening. Denial, if indulged in to an extreme degree, could become pathological. On the other hand, a certain amount of denial may actually be beneficial in helping the patient avoid excessive preoccupation with his illness. As with many behavioral phenomena, the danger is not so much a matter of kind but degree.

To help the cardiac patient who manifests these symptoms, the pastoral counselor should seek to open up a way by which the patient can explore and own his feelings. When the patient is able to verbalize his psychological processes, healing can take place. The goal of a good counseling relationship is for the patient to acknowledge reality in order to make those adjustments in his life style that are consistent with his diagnosis and prognosis. The pastoral counselor can facilitate the patient's acknowledgement of his real condition by helping create an atmosphere of acceptance and honesty while demonstrating genuine concern.

The pastoral counselor can do this in a variety of ways. Sometimes by asking the patient how others perceive his illness may allow the patient to project his anxieties and bring his real attitudes out into the open. Perhaps a direct approach might be appropriate. He might initiate a conversation beginning, "Many cardiac patients find it hard to believe that they have acutally had a heart attack. . ." In any case, the pastoral counselor stands in a position to give tremendous emotional support to the patient.

II. Phobic Reaction

The cardiac patient does have much to fear; however, his fears may be blown out of proportion and retard the therapeutic process. When he cannot cope with his fears and he becomes psychologically immobilized, his reaction can be characterized as phobic. Real fears include such things as possible recurrence of a myocardial infarction, perhaps more severe or even fatal (Lancet, 1971). In addition to this, a limitation or loss of his productivity is feared by most men who are often the only or main bread-winner. The economic ramifications in terms of hospital and medical bills and time off work may plague the patient.

As with the patient who exhibits a denial reaction, this patient also has more fear than he can handle. His reaction, although apparently opposite of denial, nonetheless has a common etiology. Each are a product of psychological anxiety.

The phobic patient has an exaggerated view of his condition. He will not be able to believe he is progressing as well as he is. He will be reluctant to resume gradually such routine tasks as shaving and feeding himself. Since he is so afraid he might overdo and have another attack, he actually malingers. He is apt to take advantage of those who are charged with his care. Even in his own home his family is imposed upon, and they are hesitant to challenge this pattern of over-dependence (Lancet, 1971).

Notwithstanding, the physician's assurances to the contrary, he will be overcautious and regard himself as being extremely fragile. No matter how favorable the prognosis, he will become a "cardiac cripple." He may become moody and withdraw from people and social events, using his heart as the reason.

As with the denial reaction, the pathology is in the over-reactive behavior. It is normal and healthy for the cardiac patient to be realistic in his appraisal of what has happened to him and accept it for what it is. In reacting to the emotional shock of having a myocardial infarction, the patient may err in going to either extreme of what could be called a self-care continuum. Diagramatically, it can be plotted in this way:

Extreme	Realistic	Extreme
Neglect	Appraisal	Indulgence
(Denial)		(Phobic)

Fig. 3 Self-Care Continuum

To relate effectively with the phobic patient, the pastoral counselor should not attempt to belittle or scorn his fears. This attack on his defense structure will only cause more anxiety and make the patient even more fearful. Ideally, his fears should be openly and frankly discussed: the irrationality of the degree of fear will subside in proportion to the emotional support the patient receives. Emotional support does not imply innocuous sympathy, but the genuine effort by the pastoral counselor to view things from the patient's perspective. Hopefully in an atmosphere of mutual esteme and trust, the patient can convince himself of the unreasonableness of the amount of fear he entertains.

Because of family visiting restrictions, the pastoral counselor becomes a very significant person to the cardiac patient. Therefore, his attitude toward the patient's condition is closely observed and picked up by the patient. A calm yet concerned approach to the meeting of his emotional needs gives the patient a model of dealing with anxiety. A genuine caring without inappropriate sentiment contributes to the reduction of the patient's fears, both real and imaginary.

III. Guilt Reaction
A seemingly inevitable concomitant of having a myocardial infarction is a guilt reaction. The patient searches for causes and reasons for the onset of his heart attack. He not only assails the physician with questions as to what in his life style is responsible for it, but he may also question his religious beliefs. In either case, the search for the etiology is an attempt to place blame on something in his way of life which he should or should not have done.

Such attempts to get a specific cause and effect relationship are futile at best and harmful at worst. It may make the patient emotionally upset and hinder his recovery when he unwholesomely dwells on the themes of "why me?" and "why now?" However, the fact that no one, single definite link between his style of life and his heart attack may be conclusively proven, may be psychologically threatening and hard to handle. This is so because it takes the possibility of another attack out of his control. He feels victimized by forces he cannot explain or manipulate.

Not only will the patient himself expend emotional energy searching out his guilt, but the patient's family will probably go through this same process. The patient's wife may think she has made too many demands upon her husband's time and energy, or that she has not provided him with a happy home free from stress, or that she has not prepared him a diet conducive to good health. These self-accusations go to the very core of the marriage relationship and cause friction and misunderstanding. The wife may become subconsciously hostile to him for these implied criticisms of her role, or she may work out her feelings of guilt in over-protecting him to compensate for her imagined neglect.

Similarly, if the patient's activities are greatly curtailed and his ability to provide materially for his family is diminished, the patient's image of himself may be shattered. If he feels he should have slowed his pace down or quit smoking sooner, ect., he may feel guilty for the economic adjustments necessary for his family. His family likewise may blame him for having to tighten their belts, then feel guilty for having such thoughts and feelings. Guilt almost seems to be contagious in the family circle, and it generally leads to depression and often despair.

IV. Depression Reaction

One of the most common reactions in a coronary care unit is that of depression (Cassem and Hackett, 1971). While this may be exacerbated by sedation, much of the patient's depression comes from attitudes held by society in general. Whatever the source, the depression is real and may be seen as an extreme reaction in antithesis to guilt. In terms of self-blame, this relationship may be plotted in this way:

Blames	Accepts	Defaults
Self	Reasonable	To "Fate"
Entirely	Responsibility	(Depression)
(Guilt)		

Fig. 4 Self-Blame Continuum

The depression may center upon a real or imagined problem in the coronary patient's current situation or may be more free-floating and nonspecific. The depth of the depression may be considered dangerously low when the patient, often in his own words, "gives up." He takes no responsibility or interest in his physical prognosis or care.

Just as the acceptance of forgiveness is therapeutic in guilt reaction, the extension of hope by the pastoral counselor is therapeutic in depression. Hope is not an unrealistic wishing process, but an expectation of the fulfillment of God's promises. Assurances made by the pastoral counselor on this basis can significantly aid the patient in working through his depression.

In dealing with the depressed patient, it is difficult for the pastoral counselor to give convincing verbal assurances to him. An inane optimism on the pastoral counselor's part may actually deepen the reaction of despondency. To be of help, the pastoral counselor should attempt to attain a level of empathy which plunges the depths of the patient's depression and sincerely shares the patient's grief. When the patient begins to tell himself that, as bad as things are, it could be worse, his attitude is moving in the right direction.

145

The pastoral counselor will appreciate the patient's grieving reaction to the loss of normal heart function. His understanding of the psychological significance of this loss places him in a position to be of great assistance in the patient's working out his sense of guilt and frustration. Again, the pastoral counselor's estimation and acceptance of the patient as a person will help immeasurably in this process.

These four reactions are perhaps the most common personality changes which are noted in the cardiac patient. A solid pastoral counseling response to these changes can contribute greatly to the patient's peace of mind and the physical progress he makes. Hopefully, an understanding of what makes the cardiac patient react the way he does, will enable the pastoral counselor to help rather than react indifferently and thus compound the psychological problems the patient already faces. It should be stressed that the pastoral counselor should be alert to those personality changes that are so extreme and profound, that psychiatric referral is indicated.

It might be noted here that the pastoral counselor often feels most inadequate in the whole area of intensive medicine. Whether in the coronary care unit, the intensive care unit, or the emergency room, he feels intimidated by the brusqueness of the medical and nursing personnel and the proliferation of technical gadgetry. He often underestimates the value of his contribution to the well-being of the patient.

However, the opposite is actually the case. While being careful not to interfere in the therapeutic efforts, the pastoral counselor should not retreat. His presence is important to both patient and staff. He should not hesitate to pray audibly for the patient if the patient is responsive; he need not feel apologetic for his part in the care of the patient. At the same time, he should always check at the nursing station to identify himself and to be given clearance for his visit.

Chapter XIV

Counseling the Cancer Patient

The disease of cancer in all its various forms affects about one in four persons in the United States at the present time ("Cancer Facts and Figures," 1975). This being the case, the number of patients with that diagnosis make up a large proportion of the hospital population. However, cancer affects virtually every system and organ of the human body with great individual differences as to the rate of growth and response to therapy. How a person responds to his or her own situation, then, will be a combination of several relevant circumstances. In order to counsel more effectively, these circumstances must be ascertained and appreciated.

It is advanced by this writer that the information received by the use of four important questions may be helpful in identifying the patient's psychological field, thus generalizations concerning the most effective pastoral counseling approach can be advanced. These questions include: (1) What is the developmental age of the patient? (2) What stage of illness is current? (3) What is known of the patient's support system? and (4) What is known of the patient's spiritual and religious resources? In the order above, these questions will be discussed, concluding with the implications for the pastoral counselor.

I. Developmental Age
The concept of developmental age is common to many psychological systems (Hurlock, 1974; Erikson, 1968). Each

divides the chronological life span into different stages with accompanying psychodynamic characteristics. For the purpose of this paper, four developmental ages will be somewhat arbitrarily assigned. They are indicated below with the appropriate chronological age.

1. Childhood - birth to 18 years.
2. Young adult - 19 to 35 years.
3. Mature adult - 36 to 69 years.
4. Old age - 70 years and on.

1. *Childhood.* It is obvious that each of these divisions could be subdivided for additional refinement. There are obvious and profound differences between a neonate and a teenager in their individual capacity to react to the disease (Kerney, 1969). However, the parental (indeed, societal) reaction is almost universally one of anger. This common denominator emerges time and time again, and the pastoral counselor can expect to deal with this emotional reaction. Perhaps it is that parents and society in general believe in the essential innocence and helplessness of children of all ages.

Statistics confirm that cancer is responsible for more deaths in the 3-14 age range than any other illness ("Cancer Facts and Figures," 1975). There seems to be a pervasive feeling of unfairness in the death of any child. This is accentuated when accompanied by frequent hospitalizations. Cancer is not very tangible and visible in terms of psychological ventilation and this adds to the frustration and anger of family members.

Ideally, the best pastoral counseling technique to employ is to encourage the family members to vent their anger by "fighting" cancer. If they are angry with God, permit their verbal expression of this without being judgmental. That is, encourage honesty in prayer. For example, the pastoral counselor might pray as follows:

148

"Father, we are confused and upset by what has happened to _____. We are upset and we sense with him disappointment, frustration, and yes, even irritation and anger with You. It's hard to understand how such a thing could happen and yet we know. . ."

and then go into prayer of affirmation.

The focus here is on counseling with the family constellation and is not concentrated on the patient directly. Often, the younger patient involved can handle the illness reasonably well and will tend to reflect the level of adjustment that significantly others achieve.

2. *Young Adult.* As the patient advances in both chronological and developmental age a greater degree of independence is evidenced. He or she becomes more involved in the decisions which affect him or her. The dominant emotional reaction during this period is bitterness. To the extent that older teens are self-determining, this reaction will be shared by them also. The idealism, dreams, and ambitions are cruelly curtailed or halted. Unrealization of future plans for the patient and the patient's dependent family compounds the bitterness and remorse at what could have been.

Family commitments at this time of life are intense and demanding financially. Young parents particularly are bitter about not being able to spend time with their families and resent the family resources being funneled into medical expenses. Beneath this is the spectre of not being around when the children grow up. Some bitterness at not being able to pursue the career or profession of choice at the pace desired is often observed.

At this point, the function of counseling is to enable the individual to reassess his life's goals and objectives and aid in any readjustment necessary. Some type of vocational rehabilitation program may need to be suggested and encouraged. As a spouse and parent, the young adult cancer patient needs to feel that his or her spouse and their children are able to cope with the disease emotionally as well as financially.

3. *Mature Adult.*During this stage of life, there is a shift away from a pre-occupation with raising a family and becoming established in a career. The bitterness and resentment of the previous stage may give way to several kinds of fear ("The Clergy and the Cancer Patient," 1975). Perhaps the fear is not so much that the cancer patient will not be able to be with his children or grandchildren, or be able to achieve his vocational dream, but the fear that he is dispensable. The demands as a parent and person are less and there is a fear that he or she is no longer needed. Having cancer compounds this fear of irrelevance.

As in the previous stage, further subdivision would yield more precision. However, each individual will pass through these periods at a different rate and chronological age. The purpose here is not to be exhaustive but to be suggestive. Rather than being definitive, this system of interrogation will hopefully produce an awareness of a possible theoretical approach to counseling with the cancer patient.

In the case of the mature adult, the emphasis of pastoral counseling should be on the integrity and worth of the individual as a fellow human being, regardless of past or present relationships. The assurance of acceptance is especially important because during this stage there is fear of rejection because of the very name and nature of the disease. This fear has been called "cancerophobia" (Finley, 1976). It is this fear which makes it difficult for some patients to use the word cancer itself. The emotional connotation of great and extensive pain is present in the thinking of many people at this time of life. At the risk of generalization, a man may fear loss of productivity whereas a woman may fear physical disfiguration.

4. *Old Age.*The last stage of life is unique in that the individual may be much more accepting of the inevitability of death in some form (Ross, 1971). This being the case, the dominant emotional theme at this time may be that of resignation. The haunted fear and terror of a previous stage gives way to a more accepting and acquiesing emotional reaction. Again, individual difference will be very profound, depending on other factors.

For some it is almost a relief to believe that the end of life may be near. Perhaps it is as if the suspense of wondering when and how death may come is over. Sometimes the prospect of being with a pre-deceased spouse again adds to the acceptance, if not anticipation, of the terminal process. The cancer then becomes a means to a desired end.

However, others may react exactly opposite and seek to "beat" the cancer. Their efforts may be as intense as those of a person of much younger age. Factors that may determine which alternative reaction will prevail include basic personality type and predisposition, family responsibilities and influences, and previous health history.

II. Stage of Illness

A second relevant issue in counseling with the cancer patient is the current stage of the illness. Generally, three stages are noted ("The Clergy and the Cancer Patient," 1975). The first is known as the initial stage in which the predominant medical emphasis is upon diagnosis. The second stage is when the diagnosis has been confirmed and the cancer is advancing. Here the medical effort is, of course, directed to therapy. The last stage, the terminal stage, the medical attention is more prognostic and analgesic. Each of these stages will be discussed in somewhat more detail.

1. *Initial Stage.*Sometimes the pastoral counselor will not be involved in this stage of the illness at all. This is because the primary emotional reaction is denial. A person is reluctant to discuss even the possibility of cancer until its

reality and presence cannot be denied. Perhaps this is just as well since this defense mechanism permits the patient to keep other more powerful feelings such as fear and dread from dominating his thinking.

The diagnostic efforts of the physician may create an atmosphere of doubt. If extensive testing in the hospital or clinic are indicated, the patient may realize the need for support from the pastoral counselor at this time. The pastoral counselor can be of immense service to the patient in encouraging and supporting the patient to consent to whatever testing and diagnostic procedures the physician deems necessary.

Hope should be continually offered that the diagnosis will be negative and no cancer will be detected. At the same time, the pastor should be alert to the possibility that the patient might use denial to the point of not facing reality. If it seems that the patient is actually fantasizing, the psychiatric referral may be indicated.

2. *Advancing Stage.* During and throughout this stage of illness when the diagnosis is confirmed as cancer, the patient will very likely slip in and out of periods of depression. This depression will ease or increase depending on the patient's perception of therapeutic success. There are three major therapeutic procedures employed to combat the spread or metastasis of the cancer. Depending upon such factors as rate of metastasis of the cancer, and general physical condition of the patient, they will be utilized separately or in combination. These therapies are (1) surgery, (2) radiation, and (3) chemotherapy ("The Clergy and the Cancer Patient," 1975).

If surgery is indicated, depression may be compounded by the use of anesthesia before and other analgesic medication following. Other than a most minor pre-cancerous condition (such as of the skin), hospitalization will be indicated. This may be frightening to the patient as well as discouraging. Generally, hospitalization for even diagnostic surgery will force the patient from denial into depression. Often as in conditions calling for a biopsy, the diagnostic and therapeutic surgery will be combined.

Sometimes following surgery, sometimes in lieu of surgery, radiation will be prescribed. Usually this can be done on an outpatient basis, but the depression is seldom lessened. Not only is the weekly (or whatever schedule) visit to the hospital a grim reminder of the disease and its intrusion into his life, but very often side effects of the radiation therapy (such as weakness) add to the depressed state.

Similarly in chemotherapy, the cancer patient may react physically as well as psychologically to the treatments. The more intense administration of anti-carcinogenic drugs usually involves hospitalization, at least in the beginning of their use. Whatever the therapeutic approach used, the general emotional reaction is that of depression. The pastoral counselor's concern and support can be a source of great encouragement during this time.

3. *Terminal Stage.* The last stage of the illness is probably as difficult for the family as the first two, perhaps more so. To the extent that the cancer patient becomes more physically dependent, the family will become more involved in his physical care. Along with this involvement, the witnessing of the physical deterioration of a loved one adds to the difficulty of this period.

Usually even the most determined efforts to believe that the cancer will somehow be checked, give way to a fear that in spite of their following the regimen of the physician the illness is not to be arrested. For some, the one-time defiant attitude erodes into a bitterness. For others, hope becomes harder and harder to maintain. For all, a certain fearfulness of pain, suffering and death (Kerney, 1969). The family will generally experience a frustration borne of their feelings of helplessness and impotency.

The pastoral counselor will often find a tendency to relate more to the family than the patient, especially as the cancer patient requires more sedation to be comfortable. Communication with the patient may become very difficult due to his general weakness. In either case, the dominant emotion to deal with is fear. This fear has many facets - fear of the unknown, of what to expect in terms of symptoms and signs of imminent death is one. Another fear may be that death will come when no family is present. Whatever fear of death the patient or his family have, will be brought to the surface at this time also. The ministry of the pastoral counselor is especially important at this crisis time to be a source of spiritual strength for all concerned.

III. Family Resources.

A third relevant question to be addressed is that of support systems. By this is meant the basic family resources and significant others who are in a position to give emotional support to the cancer patient. Generally, the support system varies according to the developmental age of the patient. As would be expected, the parents primarily comprise the support system in childhood. However, grandparents and aunts and uncles and the wider family may be extremely supporting too.

In certain instances, these significant others may equal or exceed the emotional security which the parents are able to give. Because of the high degree of psychological identification involved, the parents may become almost immobilized and be barely able to function themselves (Heffron, et al, 1973). If the child cancer patient dies, there is often marital difficulties and divorce in the offing for the parents.

Another support source in later childhood is the child's or adolescent's peer group (Heffron, 1975). A great deal of emotional strength may be derived from the relationship between the child and his or her classmates at school or a specially close friend. In adolescence particularly, the cancer patient may actually confide in a close friend rather than family. This may be because it is somehow less threatening to talk about such an emotionally charged illness to someone who is somewhat emotionally distant yet empathetic. This, then, may produce an extra strain on the family constellation. Communication may break down.

Here is where the pastoral counselor can make another important contribution in his counseling. He should be alert to the extra sensitivity of all family members during this time and even anticipate difficulties and seek to keep communication open between parent and child and also between parent and parent. As a thoroughly concerned non-family member, the pastoral counselor can help by interpreting to family members the attitude and behavior of other family members.

Because each family is symbiotically related to each other the potential for good or evil is great. A good positive family support system can enable the cancer patient to cope with his illness and therapy. A negative support system may cause the patient to give up and ignore the physical help available to him.

Just as parents are probably the single most important unit in the family support system of the child, in both adult stages the spouse assumes that role. However, in the young adult developmental age, the parents may continue to give great support, and in the mature adult age, the children may begin to give valuable aid. In old age, chidren may be the only support system the surviving spouse will have.

In each case, the emotional strain put on the family support system will be great. The pastoral counselor's role should be one of supporting both the cancer patient and the family. Sometimes a greater assistance can be rendered to the patient by helping the involved family members to relate effectively to the patient than by ministering directly to the patient. For if the patient's family support system is functioning properly, the pastoral counselor's role is greatly facilitated.

IV. Spiritual Resources.

The most obvious area of pastoral counseling is that of maximizing the cancer patient's spiritual resources. The question that needs to be answered is, "What is known of the spiritual resources available to the patient?" Perhaps the easiest way to assess these is to pose three simple questions about the patient's fath, hope and love (Kerney, 1969). These three dimensions are qualitatively different from the emotional and psychological aspects of patient care which are sometimes addressed.

1. *Faith.*To determine the presence and depth of the patient's faith, the following question can be raised: In what does he trust? That is, is the patient trusting in God or in superstition? Many patients professing faith in God may actually be trusting in a concept of benevolent fatalism. This is verbalized by the patients saying, "Whatever happens to me will be for the best." This may sound like deep religious faith (and indeed may be); however, it may represent spiritual weakness. However expressed, faith in God must include two important ingredients. These are the conviction that God is able to do anything (He is all-powerful) and the assurance that God cares (He is all loving). The delicate blending of these elements result in faith grounded in the revealed character of God. Anything less is trust in benign idolatry. God is living and loving! The task of faith is to maintain this trust in the attributes of God when the circumstances of illness tempt one to doubt His power and love.

The pastoral counselor's role in establishing or reinforcing the patient's faith can radically affect the patient's view of himself and the world of his illness. Counseling that emphasizes and builds on the patient's faith, whatever the degree, releases a dynamic force that can only be to the patient's best good. The alternative to a healthy faith is unhealthy doubt.

2. *Hope.* For what does the patient hope? This question probes into another potential spiritual force. The cancer patient's hope will probably shift according to the current stage of the illness. In the initial stage of his illness (the diagnostic stage), the patient's hope will likely be that the diagnosis is favorable. Hope will be maintained that the symptoms are explainable in terms of some other, less life-threatening diagnosis.

The patient's hope changes after the diagnosis has been confirmed and in the second or advancing stage (the therapeutic stage) his hope likely will be that the therapy will be successful. The patient will hope that the cancer has not metastisized, that the surgeon can "get all of it," that no side-effect prohibits the continued use of the chemotherapy, etc.

In the terminal stage, the cancer patient most probably will hope that he will not suffer intensely or for a long period of time. A recent poll indicated that cancer was the most feared illness of our society. This fear is linked to an erroneous belief that cancer kills all its victims slowly and painfully. The terminal cancer patient hopes that he can "go quickly and painlessly."

In each of these states, the task of the pastoral counselor is to help the patient shift hopes comfortably and appropriately. Of all people, the pastoral counselor can support the patient's hopes for a "miracle." At the same time, however, the pastoral counselor can render great assistance by helping the patient avoid "miracle cures" that sometimes prevent the patient from obtaining or maintaining proper medical attention. It will be a real service since far too many dollars are spent on false promises and quackery in our country (Brown, 1975).

3. *Love.* The spiritual power of love can be of immeasurable good to the cancer patient. It can be ascertained by the question, "What does he value?" The therapeutic power of human love can often be demonstrated in times of great anguish. If the patient's values are perverted and turned inward so that he loves himself first and only, the spiritual force of love is misdirected and ineffective. On the other hand, if his love is for others as God intends, the healing value to the patient is profound.

The pastoral counselor's role can be to direct the patient's feelings away from himself and toward the significant others in his life—toward his family support system. If selfishness and self-centeredness dominate the patient, the emotional drain on the support system becomes intolerable and thus is ultimately detrimental to the patient himself.

The love of God can be demonstrated as well as taught by the pastoral counselor as he relates to the cancer patient and his family. By not reacting defensively when anger is directed at him and seeking to serve the best interest of the patient instead of his own, the pastoral counselor can be an exemplar and ambassador of the love of God.

V. Role of the Pastoral Counselor.

The conclusion of this chapter will be devoted to a brief discussion of three specific suggestions for pastoral counseling with the cancer patient. However, these concepts can be applied in a general way to all patients who have a life-threatening illness. Cancer does not qualitatively change a person's basic personality, even though some have sought to identify a "cancer personality."

1. First of all, the pastoral counselor should be there. Whatever the stage of illness his presence should be welcomed. Particularly if the terminal stage is reached, the patient's fear of abandonment is accentuated (Barckley, 1970). Too often the family support system breaks down at this

point and people who "don't know what to say" shy away from the patient. In the hospital setting even the medical and nursing staff tend to deny even the existence of terminally ill in their care (Ross, 1971). So the pastoral counselor's visits assume a greater and greater importance. Not that frequency and length are the only standards of a caring visit. The quality of the visit is important also. Foremost is a listening attitude. A lot of verbiage is not necessary, but to be there and be accepting of the mood of the patient is mandatory. The terminally ill patient often has a fear of dying alone and does not want to be left alone for long periods of time. It can be of great good to the patient to assure him of continued care and convey the "silent sound of love."

2. A second suggestion is that the pastoral counselor should give the cancer patient in any stage and at any age ample opportunity for dialogue. This includes allowing the patient to ventilate his anger and disappointment and plunge into the depths of depression without censure. Too often the clergy, eager to project a positive attitude, try to talk the patient out of an unhealthy emotional state (such as anger or depression). This is probably because such a discussion makes the pastor or any visitor uncomfortable. However, the patient himself will often talk himself out of an unhealthy emotional attitude if given the freedom to do it in his own way and at his own rate. Frequently, the pastoral counselor makes the mistake of trying to hasten the therapeutic process and pushes the patient too fast or in the wrong direction. Again, the value of empathetic listening should not be underestimated.

Cancer has been described as God's "pie in the face" (Finley, 1976). Anger that is directed against God is better ventilated than repressed or projected upon those close to the patient. The pastoral counselor need not feel threatened or defensive by explosive anger, but recognize it as basically helpful to the patient.

159

Allowing the cancer patient to engage in dialogue can also be useful in rehabilitation counseling. The pastoral counselor's support for such groups as "Reach for Recovery" (for mastectomy patients) can be a factor in the patient's return to a normal and healthy life style. Emphasis should also be placed on the accomplishments of rehabilitated patients. Acceptance of a changed body image can be made easier with skillful pastoral counseling. It should be a natural emphasis of the pastoral counselor that human life consists of much more than a perfect physical body.

3. The sum and conclusion is that the pastoral counselor should be instrumental in helping the cancer patient celebrate life. As in any potentially life-threatening situation, the patient should be guided into appreciating the present moment. To live life abundantly means to live it fully in the now, one day at a time. With future uncertainty, the present should be enjoyed and accentuated.

A legitimate facet of pastoral counseling is helping the cancer patient anticipate a better ultimate future. The concept of eternal life can be explored with eagerness and awe. The very ongoing nature of human life and a wholesome realization that life's end is as fascinating and mysterious as its beginning are themes the pastor and patient may wish to discuss at the patient's initiation.

4. Perhaps the greatest service the pastoral counselor can render to the cancer patient is that of helping him overcome guilt. The guilt may originate from at least two sources. One is the guilt that comes from the spoken or unspoken question if the cancer could have been prevented. He may feel that he ignored one or more of the seven warning signals. Or he may feel that he is responsible by ignoring a high risk factor, such as cigarette smoking. Whatever the source, the cancer patient may be punishing himself unproductively.

The other source of guilt is more subtle and harder to identify. It comes from the conviction that the cancer is a direct punishment from God for some sinful past deed. As stated, the pastoral counselor can be instrumental in helping the cancer patient work out these guilt feelings, whatever the source. The mercy and forgiveness of God needs to be presented in a constructive and positive manner.

5. A final way in which the pastoral counselor can help the cancer patient is in according him a renewed sense of self-respect. As in the case with disfiguring surgical procedures, the patient may suffer a loss of personal integrity. Again, the pastoral counselor needs to reassure him that human life has value apart from a perfectly functioning body. This is important inasmuch as the cancer patient may feel inferior as a person because of odor associated with certain kinds of cancer. Also, he may suffer embarrassment because of incontinence or general dependence on others for his care. By this accepting attitude and manner toward the cancer patient, the pastoral counselor can help to dispel the negative self-image that often accompanies any major physical disability.

These then, are some specific ways in which the pastoral counselor can use his particular skills to help cancer patients through the distinctive emotional and spiritual trauma of their illness. To help a person cope with the many difficult adjustments which accompany a major illness is to express the love of God in the finest language.

Chapter XV

Counseling with the Orthopedic Patient

Orthopedic patients are somewhat unique in the hospital setting. Two factors distinguish them from the rest of the hospital population. For one thing, the average length of stay for orthopedic patients is generally longer than for either medical or surgical patients. Tremendous progress has been made in speeding recovery through improved surgical technique. However, patients who undergo total joint replacements, laminectomies, fracture settings or amputations, for example, are usually hospitalized longer than other surgical patients. Similarly, patients in traction, in body casts, or in braces, are often in the hospital for a longer duration than most medical patients.

Another factor which is peculiar to orthopedic patients is that they are more apt to be chronologically older than those in other acute units of the hospital. Part of the reason for this is vascular insufficiency which usually increases with advancing age (Clarke-Williams, 1974). Also, this is partly due to degenerative bone conditions of the older age group. An obvious case in point is the patient with a fractured hip who is usually an elderly person. Literally the word "orthopedic" is a combination of two Greek words. One, ortho (όρθό), means straight or without deformity, and the other, pedic (ποδός), means foot as in podiatric.

The pastoral counselor can be of great assistance to these patients. Often problem or difficult patient situations occur in the orthopedic unit because most medical hospitals are geared to the acute, relatively short-term patient. From the patient's viewpoint, hospitalization becomes boring and progress seems slow. Much encouragement and emotional support is called for. Because the time in the hospital will probably be extended, the pastoral counselor has an opportunity to build a rapport with the orthopedic patient that will be more durable than that possible with other hospitalized patients. Also because of the time factor, orthopedic patients may appreciate longer and/or more frequent visits than other hospital patients might.

Three main facets of orthopedic counseling will be noted. The first discussion will center on the problems associated with ambulation. Secondly, the psychological and spiritual aspects of orthopedic pain will be explored. Lastly, the emotional and spiritual support necessary in the rehabilitation of the orthopedic patient will be examined.

I. Ambulation and the Orthopedic Patient.

Man is distinguished from lower forms of life in his ability to walk erect. Part of being fully human is ambulation. Society expects each member to have this physical characteristic, and society implicity penalizes those who do not. Curbs and stairs are designed only for the walking. Car accelerators and brakes are designed only for those with normal leg use. The non-walking minority often faces severe discrimination in the design and manufacture of buildings and automobiles. The problems this poses for the paraplegic, for example, are devastating, not only physically but psychologically as well (Mazzola and Jacobs, 1973).

Society is also cruel in its emphasis upon physical perfection. Perhaps not since ancient Greece has there been such an emphasis on physical beauty and strength. Professional models and professional athletes are among the highest paid segment of our society. This being the case, the orthopedic patient has a double burden. Not only is the illness painful and confining, but the emotional side-effects are often staggering (Martin, 1976). The pastoral counselor can be of immense help in the adjustment necessary for the orthopedic patient to accept whatever limitations he might possess. Non-ambulatory patients which the pastoral counselor will contact may be of two types: (1) those with spinal cord injuries, and (2) amputees. The particular problems each of these facets will be discussed next.

A. *Spinal Cord Injuries.* The problem of those patients who have never ambulated, such as the spina bifida patient whose condition is due to congenital defect, will have a special set of emotional problems. These problems will likely center in the area of self-worth. Because this patient was never able to have the physical ability to walk, his estimation of his own value may be very low. Depending upon the style of parenting, he may be very dependent and demanding, which is a product of low self-esteem. This person may be a difficult hospital patient and will need a great deal of assurance and positive regard from the pastoral counselor, tempered with a firmness which will, hopefully, lead to greater independence and self-reliance.

Patients who, through accident or other trauma to the spinal cord, lose the use of their legs, face very difficult emotional repercussions. The loss of an ability, like the loss of a significant organ, is to be grieved and mourned for (Krup, 1976 and Steger, 1976). Progress in the counseling process can be made when the patient is allowed to go through the grief process at his own rate. The pastoral counselor's role is to encourage and permit this to happen, not only for the patient himself but also for those emotionally near him.

Those patients who are rendered non-ambulatory as a

165

result of a trauma, such as an auto accident or fall, likewise will experience a profound sense of loss. However, a loss that comes as a result of illness may be somewhat easier to accept than that which comes as a result of trauma. In cases of trauma, the patient may have a more tangible object of anger than in the case of an illness. For example, his injury and loss may be personified by a drunken driver or a faulty piece of equipment. Counseling with a patient in this situation may involve giving him more opportunity for ventilation of overt anger than those incapacitated by an impersonal disease.

B. *Amputees.* The orthopedic patient who has had one or both of his lower extremities amputated may be either temporarily or permanently non-ambulatory. At best, the patient may be able to walk with the help of a prosthesis alone or with the use of crutches or cane. Amputation is a procedure which, though necessary, causes great difficulty in adjustment. The main task of the pastoral counselor is to assure the individual patient of their wholeness as a person in the face of a significant loss and extend to them a realistic hope.

The degree of difficulty in adjusting to amputation varies from patient to patient. Generally speaking, the age and sex of the patient and the medical reason for the amputation will affect the adjustment process (Caine, 1973). The younger the patient, the more traumatic the loss; however, the resilient and flexible nature of youth tempers this in time. The older patient may actually have more fear of the future and more feelings of helplessness because they live alone or perhaps live with a spouse whose health is declining. The younger patient may regret giving up sports and dancing, and may be more negatively sensitive to the cosmetic appearance of the prosthesis. A young woman would be expected to grieve the loss of appearance, and a young man grieve the loss of strength and function.

Adequate explanation of the medical condition which

precipitated the need for amputation is a factor in acceptance also (Friedman, 1975). Amputations which are the result of an accident might be expected to engender more anger, for example, than amputations which are necessary to save the patient's life, as in diabetic or gangrenous conditions. In the latter instance, the amputation conceivably might be regarded as a life-saving blessing instead of a debilitating curse caused by an avoidable accident.

Whatever the age or sex of the patient or the medical reason for amputation, the role of the counselor is the same. It revolves around giving the patient an assurance that the change in his body's appearance and function need not affect his feelings of personal integrity and worth. A human being is more than an animal with the ability to walk erect. The humanness of an individual is a spiritual quality, and the pastoral counselor is in a unique position to stress this reality.

II. Emotional Needs of the Orthopedic Patient

Because excessive dosages of narcotic drugs used to control the pain of the orthopedic patient can produce medication dependency, many patients experience more or less chronic pain (Swanson, *et al*, 1976). Medical and hospital personnel, while dedicated to the alleviation of suffering, become concerned when the orthopedic patient's threshold for pain steadily declines. The pastoral counselor may be able to help in breaking the chain of stronger and stronger dosages of pain medication by giving a great deal of empathy and emotional support to the orthopedic patient.

Because the rate of physical progress is often slow, the patient tends to become anxious. This anxiety may well exacerbate the perception of pain and increase his requests for medication. Most medications, while controlling pain, result in a depressive affect. Since the original anxiety is not resolved, the patient continues to need "something for

167

pain." The hospital staff may become less sympathetic and this creates yet more anxiety on the part of the patient. An understanding of the dynamics involved can make the pastoral counselor sensitive to the need for a great deal of encouragement to allay both the anxiety as well as the depression many orthopedic patients experience (Farrell, 1976).

Particularly in the case of the young male orthopedic patient, recognition of sexual needs by the pastoral counselor is important (Pfefferbaum and Pasnau, 1976). Confinement in bed over a period of several weeks may produce anxiety related to sexual potency. Close physical contact with young female nurses and aides may compound the problem. An appreciation of the lack of normal sexual expression and the realization of the necessity some type of sublimation can make the pastoral counselor more empathetic and understanding of the patient's situation. Often the patient will make jokes and innuendos as a means of allaying his anxiety. Accurate interpretation of this type of behavior is an important asset to the counselor. The degrees of sexually related anxiety will vary according to the patient's age and marital status and also to the perceived duration of confinement.

In addition to anxiety over the slow rate of recuperation and sexual function, the orthopedic patient, particularly the family breadwinner, may have job-related anxieties. For example, financial concerns over loss of work, job insecurity, payment of medical and hospital costs, may all contribute to making one uncomfortable (Swanson, 1976). The young mother has anxieties born of her concern for the care of her small children, and also she may be concerned about being a drain on the family's finances. Older patients are anxious about the extent of their Medicare coverage. Financial anxieties are an almost universal phenomenon except in the case of the very young—then their parents bear the strain.

The pastoral counselor can be of help in dealing with the anxiety by helping the orthopedic patient sort out what are

168

and what are not legitimate worries. After this is done, concrete steps can be taken to enable the patient to handle specific situations and to encourage him to do as much for himself as possible. The counselor needs to be careful not to do for the patient what the patient can reasonably do for himself. To reinforce a dependent role is doing the patient no favor.

III. Rehabilitation of the Orthopedic Patient.

The goal of orthopedic medicine is that the patient recover the health and use of his bones and joints. Physical and occupational therapy figure prominently in the patient's reaching that goal. Re-learning to walk, sit, stand, etc., after weeks and even months of inactivity and disuse is difficult. It is easy to become discouraged when progress seems so slow in performing tasks once taken for granted. Not only is there physical pain in using a prosthesis, but there is often the related problem of fear.

Fear of falling and re-injuring the afflicted limb or the "good leg" is very real for most orthopedic patients (Clarke-Williams, 1974). This fear is inhibiting and consciously or subconsciously keeps a patient from expending that maximum effort that is needed to make good progress. The contribution of the pastoral counselor at this time can help the person overcome this kind of fear. By creating an accepting atmosphere in which the patient can own and express the haunting fear that plagues him, the counselor has helped to defuse some of the negative energy utilized in any phobic reaction.

Probably the greatest problem encountered in the rehabilitation of the orthopedic patient is that of discouragement (Steger, 1976). Progress often comes slowly and often there are complications and setbacks. Discouragement and depression and impatience go hand in hand, and the task of the pastoral counselor is to endeavor to keep the patient's morale boosted. A positive attitude toward exercise and physical therapy sessions will be reflected in greater effort which will produce better performance which reinforces a positive attitude (Hutterer and Denes, 1975). Conversely, a negative attitude will prevent the patient from putting forth the best effort and progress will be negligible, and this will reinforce the negative attitude.

The pastoral counselor can be of service by helping the patient to have a realistic appreciation of the small amount of progress that may be forthcoming. If a patient has unrealistic goals and expectations, there is bound to be discouragement. Further, the counselor can help by accepting the patient as a person regardless of his degree of mobility and rehabilitation progress (Weikel, et al, 1974). Approval for the patient as a person must never be conditional on his efforts or performance. However, sincere expressions of pleasure on the patients achieving those levels of proficiency that signify healing progress should not be withheld.

Whenever, in the course of the orthopedic patient's rehabilitation, there is regression, the pastoral counselor should be there to give a spiritual lift in the form of hope (Friedman and Friedman, 1975). This does not simply mean a flippant "you'll do better next time" approach. Hope acknowledges the gravity of the situation and does not gloss over the discouraging aspects of a circumstance lightly. Hope is a positive, optimistic appraisal of a serious condition. Hope for a good recovery must be maintained throughout the rehabilitation process. The counselor must not try to convince the patient he should have hope or try to infuse his own hope into the individual. The skill of counseling at this point consists of letting the patient be free to discover and express his own positive aspirations, without superimposition. Many times counselors are too quick to point out the positive aspects of a bad situation. By allowing the patient to come to recognize these on his own, even a small degree of hope will be much more convincing and real to him.

IV. Conclusion.

In this treatment of pastoral counseling with the orthopedic patients, the physical problems peculiar to them have been briefly examined. The emotional responses typical to physical debilitation have been outlined. Discussion has centered on the ambulation, amputation and rehabilitation of the orthopedic patient. Attention has been given to the problems of pain, a negative self-image and discouragement as these relate to the orthopedic patient. Hopefully, an implicit counseling approach based on acceptance of the patient as a person and the importance of genuine empathy for that person has been conveyed also.

Chapter XVI

Counseling the Psychiatrically Depressed Patient

There is some debate on the appropriate depth and extent of pastoral counseling in a psychiatric setting. Even as other health professionals need a psychiatric residency to be qualified to work with emotionally disturbed patients, the pastoral counselor should have clinical training and experience with this type of patient before attempting any in-depth counseling. At the same time, the trained pastoral counselor should not abdicate his role or underestimate the therapeutic impact of his relationship with his patient.

Since many medical hospitals have a psychiatric unit, and since many psychiatric patients manifest depression as a primary symptom, the discussion here will center on counseling with the depressed patient. The following issues will be addressed: (1) What is depression? (2) How is depression expressed? (3) What is the role of the pastoral counselor?

Before engaging in this discussion a brief examination of the psychiatric unit is in order. Generally speaking, patients in this area of the hospital differ from other hospital patients in relation to visiting regulations and movement within the hospital.

The regulation of visitors is at the discretion of the psychiatrist who may decide that the patient's problem may be magnified by social contacts and may limit or advise against even the patient's family visiting, at least initially. This being the case, the pastoral counselor should check with the head nurse or physician as to the timing of his visits. On the other hand, the patient's physician may opt for encouraging social contact. Depending in part on the physician's perception of the etiology of the patient's illness, he will decide what he feels is in the patient's best interest. At no time does the pastoral counselor want to contribute to the distress of the patient, so he should respect the judgment of those entrusted with the primary care of the patient.

In the same way, the patient's movement within the hospital may be limited. While it is not at all likely that any unit ever be locked, psychiatric patients may be restricted to their own unit. The need for more constant care for those with less grasp of reality is apparent. With the current use of drug therapy, however, it is highly unlikely that physical restraint is ever needed. More typical is the patient who has working privileges and goes and comes from the unit by mutual agreement.

I. What is Depression?

There is always an inherent danger in the assigning of labels to any form of mental illness. Depression is no different in this regard (Schuyler, 1975). Everyone becomes depressed at times, so the psychiatrically depressed patient must be distinguished by degree than by occurence. Depression becomes a clinical concern when there seems to be no apparent causation, and it persists to the point of being an abiding emotional affect.

From a diagnostic viewpoint, psychotic depression may be one of alternating states of consciousness as in the manic-depressive patient (Freedman, et al, 1972). This depression may last from a relatively short time to a much longer period, but may give way to a manic phase with little or no warning. The schizophrenic patient who is depressive

174

will manifest the same symptoms, but is not given to any self-blame and self-reproach (Freedman, et al, 1972). Both these types of depression may be so profound and abiding that institutionalization of long duration and extensive psychotherapy are usually indicated. Therefore, this type of patient would not be seen in the medical hospital psychiatric unit as a general rule.

The depressive patient in the hospital's psychiatric unit will more likely be acute and short-term. The depression will usually be related to rather specific life situations. A common pattern, for example, would be a patient in a depressed state, who overdoses because of traumatic marital problems. In the wake of an emotionally devastating divorce, a person may become very depressed.

Also, depression is almost always present in time of loss of a body function, of a close family member, or of any relationship or object which is significant and symbolic (Mendels, 1970). As indicated, the duration of this type of depression may be relatively brief and not indicative of any deep-seated psychiatric maladjustment. It is in reaction to adverse circumstances. Profound psychotic depression will be more "free-floating" and less identifiable with anything specific in the patient's personal or social psychological field.

Although the intensity of symptoms of depression will vary from patient to patient, there are a number of recurring symptoms that characterize the depressed patient. Attempts to rate and scale these characteristics have resulted in a number of instruments designed to measure depression. One, for example, uses physical symptoms—loss of weight, vomiting and pain—as references. Another uses the following items: Beyond weeping; Weeping does not relieve; Weeping relieves; Weeps frequently; Feels will not get better; Fluctuation of mood; Everything hopeless; Weeps occasionally; Feels depressed obviously (Gallant and Simpson, 1976). The frequency of occurence and intensity of these and other related symptoms will give the pastoral counselor some insight into the nature and severity of depression in the patients he contacts.

II. How is Depression Expressed?

The expression of depression can be quite varied. The pastoral counselor should not limit his thinking to the sad, melancholic, stereotype. A recent concept, "masked depression" (Leese, 1974) makes it clear that depression may be seen in more behaviors than psychosomatic disorders. A case is made for depression being disguised by deviant sexual behavior, outburts of temper, accident proneness, and various anti-social acts.

In a recent monograph (Enelow and Weinstein, 1973) the point is made that patients who manifest anxiety as an apparent syndrome may actually be suffering from depression. Referring to depression as one of the "great masqueraders", they point out the symptomatology of depression may be hidden by smiles, physical complaints, and behavioral disturbances. They distinguish between "reactive depression" which have some clear precipitating cause and an "endogenous depressions" in which there are no clear precipitating factors. The first are considered neurotic depressions, and the latter are considered psychotic depressions. Depression is viewed as being on a continuum rather than as a punctiliar entity.

As mentioned, depression is expressed in a variety of behaviors, and the pastoral counselor will see it in patients who are suicidal. The self-destructive patient has been discussed elsewhere, but it should be noted at this point that depressive symptoms often precede a suicidal gesture.

Another type of patient who manifests depression is the alcoholic patient. The alcoholic patient is often seen at the medical hospital because of the physical damage resulting from alcohol abuse. Many hospitals have a detoxification

176

unit where the alcoholic patient is "dried-out". Most alcoholic treatment programs are in separate facilities such as a state hospital. Alcoholism is considered by many as a disease rather than a perversion and is treated accordingly.

Ironically, the alcoholic patient uses that drug to ward off depression. Even though alcohol is a pharmacological depressant, it may temporarily relieve feelings of dejection and depression. But, as Milt (1976) comments, "Drinking may exacerbate an existing state of anxiety or depression . . ." A vicious cycle which is self-continuing thus develops.

Since depression wears many hats, the pastoral counselor should be alert to the possibility that depression may be an underlying factor in the patients he contacts in other, non-psychiatric areas of the hospital. Depression is often a post-surgical phenomenon, particularly in open-heart patients. Often the reaction to the administration of a general anesthetic is one of depression. Again it should be noted that depression will be encountered frequently in patients in the general medical hospital on a temporary basis and should be expected. The depression which is pathological is encountered in a psychiatric unit and is more abiding. Pastoral counseling with the depressed patient will be discussed below.

III. What is the Pastoral Counselor's Role

If the patient is in the psychiatric unit of the hospital, the pastoral counselor should, of course, check with the physician or nurse to determine if a pastoral visit is in order. Care must be taken to assure the medical and nursing staff of the competency and contribution of the pastoral counselor in functioning as a member of a healing team. A therapeutic counseling session will be characterized by giving the patient permission to expression his/her depression without judgment.

Depression may have religious overtones. As Smithe

177

(1972) says: "One common complaint of the depressed person . . . is that he has lost his faith. He can't pray or worship, has no sense of the presence of God in his life." Also, the patient may genuinely feel that God has abandoned him because of some real or imagined misdeed. The pastoral counselor need not feel compelled to defend God or try to convince the patient that his perceptions are theologically faulty. The patient may feel he is beyond redemption and that God no longer cares about Him or answers his prayers.

The pastoral counselor can assist the patient out of depression by allowing the patient to verbalize the depths of his religious despair and assuring that patient that he understands why the patient feels as he does. Since the patient may already hold an erroneous view of God's relation to himself, it is important that the pastoral counselor convey a nonjudgmental attitude.

Since very often the patient's guilt accompanies or enhances his depression, the pastoral counselor must listen carefully for clues to this complicating condition (Mendels, 1970). Very often the depression that follows the loss of a spouse or child is tied in with the belief that the survivor could have or should have done something more or said something more that might have changed the course of unfavorable outcome of an accident or illness. The reasoning process may be impaired by grief to the extent that the survivor has some very unreal concepts of his influence in the causative process. A classic example of this is the wife who may have been out shopping or other legitimate errand while her husband suffered a fatal heart attack at home.

The pastoral counselor may be able to lead the depressed into an acceptance of the love and forgiveness of God in a constructive and therapeutic process. By virtue of the imparted authority which is often conferred upon a pastoral figure, the patient may be able to accept the forgiveness of the God the pastoral counselor represents. The pastoral counselor may enable the depressed patient to focus any anger that is turned inward to appropriate and realistic expression and act as an objective sounding board for that anger.

To the extent that the pastoral counselor can create and sustain such a relationship with the depressed patient, will be the extent of the help given. For the relationship, as in any psychotherapy, assumes a greater importance than the implicit or explicit psychological theory or technique which the pastoral counselor may personally embrace. To lead a person to an acceptance of themselves as an inherently valuable child of God—the object of God's great love in Christ-is to unleash a great tremendous healing force within himself.

From such a sublime role the pastoral counselor may also be involved in such mundane matters as acting as liaison between the patient and his family, particularly if visiting privileges are limited. He may also help in explaining the need for such regulations to the patient and/or his family. Often just in his "being there" and evincing concern and a willingness to help, the love and presence of God are interpreted to the depressed patient and his family.

Chapter XVII

Counseling the Terminally Ill Patient

Currently, largely due to the efforts of Dr. Elisabeth Kubler-Ross, the subject of death and dying is no longer taboo. The impact of her contribution to the care of terminally ill will be felt for generations to come. A possible analogy may be made between her research and writing and that of Sigmund Freud in that each broke down existing barriers to open discussion and investigation. Neither have employed pure empirical methods of research, and both have been criticized accordingly. However, it cannot be denied that neither sex or death are now off limits in terms of lay interest and (perhaps) exploitation.

Because of the popularization of death as a legitimate subject of inquiry, there has been a plethora of books, articles, tapes, etc. in this field. There is a danger that death and dying, like sex, may become overworked and abused in ways unintended by professionals like Kubler-Ross. Even though she cautions against using her five stages of terminal illness as an absolute concept, Kubler-Ross' formulation will necessarily be misunderstood and inappropriately applied by some.

Reaction to the sudden emergence of well-intentioned "experts" has already set in. Hudson (1978) refers to the current situation as the "zealous phase." He is concerned that the issues involved are more complex than the sometimes simplistic approach used by many. In a similar vein, Vanderpool (1978) suggests that death with dignity may not be an ethical ideal after all and proposes dying with a sense of worth to be a better guideline.

There is, of course, a need for the pastoral counselor to be aware of possible abuses in dealing with the terminally ill patient. Sensitivity to the patient as a full person is the beginning of relating to the needs of the terminally ill. This type of sensitivity implies an acceptance that does not seek to impose any psychological system upon the counseling relationship.

In this chapter three areas of counseling with the terminally ill patient will be examined. These are (1) Dealing with Anticipatory Grief, (2) Dealing with Unresolved conflicts and (3) Dealing with Religious Anxiety. A treatment of the classic five stages of terminal illness is contained in Chapter X—Counseling with Families of the Stillborn Infant. Prolongation of life is discussed at length in Chapter VIII.

I. Anticipatory Grief

When death comes suddenly with no warning, a person has no anticipatory grief, per se. However, any reflection on one's own mortality and finitude might be construed as a form of anticipatory grief. The term usually is employed to describe the grieving a person experiences when confronted with the diagnosis of a terminal illness. Terminal illness simply refers to the inefficacy of medical or surgical intervention to restore the patient to even a modicum of health. Dying, as a process, is the eventual inability of the body to restore or replenish its cellular structure. Death is the eventual, inevitable cessation of all bodily functions. Great debate has taken place in precisely defining and describing these concepts in detail, but the reality of death and dying is essentially non-debatable. (Pollock, 1978).

The pastoral counselor needs to be aware of the precise clinical and legal definition of death to make ethical decisions accordingly. Organ donation would be a possible case in point. In addition to a somewhat academic and intellectual approach to death, the pastoral counselor needs to be aware of his own emotional reaction to death. This is necessary to comprehend and empathize with the dying patient. A keen appreciation of one's own finitude is certainly a Biblical concept. ("Teach us to number our days. . .," "It is appointed to man once to die," "The time of my departure is come," "A time to be born, a time to die," etc.)

Whenever the pastoral counselor can identify with and see himself in the person of the dying patient, he is in a position to listen appreciatively and counsel effectively. A part of the anguish of the dying person is the feeling of isolation and loneliness. To know that another person comprehends even a portion of his grief is a source of help and strength to the dying patient. The grief that the dying patient works through himself has been called "anticipatory grief," and is similar to the grief process the family may experience later on.

The key concept in death is loss. Life is a series of losses and death is the final and irretrievable loss. Much of the maturing process consists of coping with losses (as well as gains), and in this sense, Kubler-Ross refers to death as the "final stage of growth" (1975). Helping the person work through to an acceptance of death as the profound loss in a life characterized by other major and minor losses is an important contribution to the patients' emotional well-being. The message of the Christian gospel is that death is not the final goal and destiny of man's existence or essence. The Apostle Paul's faith was such that he conceives death as gain (Phil. 1:21). To accept death as genuine loss and yet accept death as an ultimate gain is a delicate balance for anyone to obtain. The pastoral counselor will not want to deny or minimize the concept of loss to the dying patient and family, yet he has an obligation to extend a real assurance of eternal life in Christ at the same time.

It must not be implied that faith in the eternal realities be substituted for the cathartic and therapeutic benefit of the grief process, but neither should the legitimate comfort of Scripture be denied anyone.

II. Unresolved Conflicts

Kubler-Ross (1969, 1975) uses the phrase "unfinished business" to describe an integral part of the grief process. The role of the pastoral counselor is to enable the terminally ill patient to move as smoothly as possible into and through this aspect of the dying process. Great care should be exercised not to push a patient in this direction at the risk of seeming to remove any hope of recovery; at the same time the pastoral counselor should be quick to respond and assist the patient and try not to talk them out of it. Since death is inevitable for all, a discussion of funeral arrangements, disposition of assets need not be construed as a morbid or defeatist activity.

A patient's unfinished business implies more than attention to these somewhat mundane matters. Often of great importance may be relationships which need to be healed before the patient lapses into a condition which precludes any efforts in this direction. As Bowers, et al (1975) expressed it: "The goal of the counseling process is to help the patient find in his own terms a completeness for his life, a meaning for his being that is not obliterated by the prospect of his non-being." Part of this completeness involves resolving any inter-personal conflicts that may set the stage for pathological grief after the patient expires.

This means that the pastoral counselor must be aware of any family dynamics that are disturbing to the patient. As an agent and proclaimer of man's reconciliation to God, the

184

pastoral counselor can also be an agent and proclaimer of man's reconciliation to others. Usually these kinds of needs are encountered within the inner circle of one's family. Spouse and spouse or children and spouse will be the most commonly fractured relationships that may bring great distress to the dying before death and to the bereaved after death. Often the task of comforting the bereaved can be best facilitated by helping them and the patient work out any hostility and alienation that has separated families.

Unhappily this may not always be possible and then a great deal of guilt may be encountered by both patient and family. The task of the pastoral counselor will be a considerable one at this point. It is the opinion of this writer that some degree of guilt is almost inevitable in even the best of family relationships. The fallibility and imperfection of human nature dictates this. There is always something one regrets saying or not saying, doing or not doing that can never be rectified after death. To lead the patient and family in the granting and accepting of forgiveness is one of the finest contributions the pastoral counselor can make to the healing of unresolved conflicts.

Many of a patient's unresolved conflicts revolve around a sense of incompleteness in terms of personal accomplishments and self-development as well as that of impaired inter-personal relationships. A healthy sense of self-acceptance by the patient should be one goal of pastoral counseling. At a time when acceptance by the outside world becomes irrelevant, self-acceptance becomes paramount. As Rosenthal (in Ruitenbeek, 1973) observes: ". . . The dying patient has no future, but the therapist can deal with his past and try to eradicate or diminish feelings of worthlessness and futility." Again to give assurance of God's forgiveness and acceptance can be of great value in helping a person achieve a real sense of wholeness and self-acceptance.

185

III. Religious Anxiety

It is difficult to distinquish between the overlapping anxieties that overtake the dying patient. It is somewhat academic to differentiate between the emotional and spiritual domain. However, many patients manifest distinct fears about their relationship to God. One large area of help the pastoral counselor can give the terminally ill is in their achieving a place with God. This help may come in the form of prayer (Lucas, 1978), and spiritual counseling.

It goes without saying that the pastoral counselor will not impose his personal theological beliefs upon the patient. However, care should be taken not to abdicate his responsibility as a representative of the Divine. There is sometimes overreaction and aversion to "deathbed conversion" so that the pastoral counselor may be too hesitant to explore fully religious problems and questions the patient might have. Such overreaction is disasterous when it prevents a dying person from obtaining that sense of spiritual peace and well-being which comes from having a right relationship with God.

One thing the pastoral counselor will need to do is to listen carefully for and to expressions of religious concern. The dying patient may be a person of deep faith and commitment who in physical duress, experiences a sense of abandonment by God. Such a person may feel he has "lost his faith" when he has doubts about the reality of God in his life. Most often this type of patient needs reassurance of the unchanging character of God's love and grace and needs to be reminded that faith and feeling are not necessarily synonymous.

Other religious anxieties may center around past misdeeds. This patient may feel that they are beyond redemption. Sometimes the guilt they experience emerges from long periods of self-examination and a judgmental review of their entire life. As the late Carl Nighswonger (1972) writes: "The

186

badness and unworthiness which he feels convinces him that he is getting what he deserves. Or the alienation from others which he experiences in his depressive withdrawal becomes so intense that he concludes, 'What's the use?' In either case, the drama ends in spiritual bankruptcy." Sometimes the patient may need help in accepting forgiveness. Again the role of the pastoral counselor will be supportive, and he will give to the patient the reassurances of God's redeeming purpose in Christ, regardless of the real or perceived magnitude of personal sin.

The pastoral counselor should also be sensitive to the importance of sacramental symbolism to the terminally ill patient. Without imparting his own theological interpretation to either baptism or communion, he may minister to the sacramental needs of the patient to the extent the patient invests him with that authority. He may need to confer with the patient's family concerning such administration, depending upon the patient's age and church background. At appropriate times the assurance of the pastoral counselor's participation in the funeral service may be a source of comfort to the patient and family also.

Of supreme spiritual help, and the foundation of Christian ministry, is the comfort and succorance of the Scripture. Particularly those passages relating to the resurrection of Christ can sustain and give great consolation to the dying patient and his family. Readings in Psalms and other passages which emphasize the eternal on-going purposes of God and his love and purpose for each individual are very appropriate also.

Above all, the very presence and understanding of the pastoral counselor should not be underestimated. Showing concern and compassion is the highest form of service to another human being. By exhibiting a sensitivity that creates an atmosphere of understanding and empathy, the religious anxieties of the patient can be addressed and mollified.

Summary

A great deal of material has emanated from psychiatric and counseling perspectives about death and dying. Because of his identification and calling the pastoral counselor is uniquely equipped to be of great assistance to the dying person and his family. Dealing with anticipatory grief, unresolved conflicts and religious anxiety, the pastoral counselor meets a need other health professionals cannot. While the focus of this chapter has been primarily upon the patient, many of these concepts and principles may be applied when dealing with the family of the terminally ill patient.

Chapter XVIII

Counseling the Geriatric Patient

The increase in number and proportion of the aging in our national population is a well-documented phenomenon (Hiltner, 1975). This trend is expected to extend well into the next century. While the South and Southwest are expected to absorb increasing numbers of retirees, the distribution of the aging in America is endemic. Much needed attention is being given at the national level in terms of meeting the physical and social needs of the aging American. The focus of this chapter, however, will be on the spiritual needs of the geriatric patient.

The relevance of such an examination is borne out in the Louis Harris poll of 1975, which reports:

> *"Seventy-one percent of the public 65 and over feels that religion is very important in their own lives, compared with only 49% of those under 65."*

While it may be that statistics will not continue to reflect religious interest and advancing years, the present numbers of older persons for whom religion is very relevant makes it a legitimate avenue of discussion. Therefore, the purpose of this chapter is to explore the specific spiritual needs of the geriatric patient in the hospital population. Three main topics will be discussed: 1) The need for faith, 2) The need for hope, and 3) The need for love. These three spiritual needs are universal; their application here is only to the aging.

I. The Need for Faith

The particular life circumstances of the aging make the need for faith paramount. So much that happens in the aging years tests one's faith to the ultimate. The need for spiritual reassurance and stability in time of debilitating change is great. So often the traditional sources of such assurances are inaccessible to the aging. It becomes difficult if not impossible to participate in church and parish life due to health problems. One's spouse may not be able to be supportive, and the loss of one's spouse may contribute to the very loneliness and hurt for which a special measure of faith is needed. This can be a cruel cycle indeed.

The financial crunch of reduced income and increasing medical and hospital costs is another source of anxiety for which faith is needed. It is apparent that the aging cannot use work as an outlet or release from the anxiety that being out of work creates. This may produce another cruel cycle. Particularly in the light of current inflationary trends the economic situation of many aging persons is just cause for concern and fear for their future. To trust God is eminently important at such a time and the pastoral counselor needs to affirm this.

Another source of affirmation which is often denied the aging is society itself. Social ostracism is often encountered by the aging in a culture which deifies youth. This can result in self-effacement, an almost apologetic attitude on the part of the aging whose only sin is that they have managed to survive over the years. The triumph is bittersweet at best, and the aging's faith in society is often shaken or shattered. A sense of belonging—of community—may be denied those who need this support the most.

The loss of independence that often accompanies advancing age is another developmental aspect that makes faith such an important spiritual dimension. Particularly if loss of independence means giving up one's home and being institutionalized, there a serious adjustment crisis. The pastoral counselor needs to impart a great deal of spiritual support in the difficult transitions which face the aging. Faith in God's providence, in society, in one's family and one's self are all important ingredients in coping with the life style changes which go along with aging in our culture. The pastoral counselor can be helpful as a part of the geriatric patient's support system during hospitalization.

Faith is the antidote for fear, anxiety and despair. It answers the deep need for persons of all ages who face a deteriorating physical situation. To trust implicitly in the goodness of God when the familiar world one has grown accustomed to is crumbling requires not only inner strength but also a good deal of "outer" help from the pastoral counselor.

II. The Need for Hope

In addition to faith, the geriatric patient needs hope. As a person grows older death seems more inevitable. Friends and family members pass away with increasing frequency. Physical ills come more often and are more serious and result in frequent hospitalization. Death is never a respector of age, but as an old adage expresses it, "The young do die; the old must die." This being the case the need for some preparation for death is called for.

The essence of the Christian faith centers about the death and resurrection of Jesus Christ. This belief produces hope for an ultimate future. The nature of hope is that its perspective is beyond the present into the future. The future of the aging is not pleasant. In addition to deterioration of health, faculties and senses and the resulting decline in physical appearance, many other losses face the aging. Losses in the aging years are more permanent and difficult to replace. Loss of one's mate is often the most crushing blow.

191

For what can the aging reasonably hope? Hope shifts from the mundane concerns to the more ultimate realities. It no longer makes sense to hope for perfect physical health. Hope centers immediately on continuing to live as independently as possible. When and if independence is lost, hope transfers its goal to living as pain-free as possible. When and if this hope fails, the aging simply hopes for a quick and dignified death.

Because at least the majority of the present generation of aging persons regard religion as important, hope for eternal life is very real. As Green and Simmons (1977) express it:

> *"Yet it is the hope that Christ promises of eternal life that allows one to hold on to the thread of meaningful existence at the door of the greatest threat to all meaning-death."*

This kind of hope is the antithesis of existential despair that finds no meaning or purpose in living at any chronological age.

Loss of meaning and purpose can be a real spiritual problem of the aging. Particularly if one reviews the past and sees only the lack of personal fulfillment. To extend to such a one a new future and beginning in the form of hope in a better hereafter is to meet such a spiritual need. The pastoral counselor must extend hope in the time of death as an antidote for the guilt and depression which is often encountered.

III. The Need for Love

"Faith, hope, love - and the greatest of these is love" (1 Corinthians 13). The single, most important need of all humanity is for love, and geriatric patients are certainly no exception. Love is the essential factor in self-actualization and personality integration. Love is a social concept in that it requires an object outside one's own self. Thus it is a relational experience between persons. Usually, relationships within the family are the most important and such relationships help give one a sense of personal worth. Our very reality and integrity as a person is attested when one loves and is loved.

As indicated the geriatric patient needs this affirmation from the pastoral counselor as much or perhaps more than other patients. Characteristically in our culture the aging have fewer contacts outside the family constellation because of employment retirement and lessened mobility. However, the aging years are those in which family members and social peers are taken by death. The loss of one's spouse and all the personal and social relationships connected therewith are often suddenly, irrevocably severed.

The ensuing isolation and loneliness can lead to a loss of personal identity. Thus another vicious cycle is set in motion. At a time when one needs love the most, the sources of that love are often lost. The cause of one's grief is at the same time the loss of one's comfort. It is a difficult blow from which to recover.

Added to this is the loss of identity that occurs when one "retires" from a life vocation. Our culture too closely identifies work with worth and productivity with power. When, in the aging years, one loses other relationships the loss of prestige that accompanies work retirement comes as a severe blow also. Our work ethic dictates that cessation of one's career as loss. It is not necessarily idle chatter to speak of "loving" a job. Too often adequate preparation for this adjustment is not made.

Love is unconditional acceptance and, though its source is God, the pastoral counselor should be its channel. When one is limited in relationships with significant others, personality disintegration will follow. Aging persons, all persons, need love and the accompanying sense of self-worth. Ideally the pastoral counselor can be a vehicle to transmit

God's love to the aging to insure spiritual health and well being in time of physical distress.

Conclusion

Bringing together the spiritual needs of faith, hope and love for the aging, the goal of spiritual well-being can be achieved. A useful definition of spiritual well-being was developed in interfaith study in 1975 (Clingan, 1978). The statement is:

"Spiritual well-being is the affirmation of life in a relationship with God, self, community and environment that nurtures and celebrates wholeness."

To enhance and enable spiritual well-being in the lives of those of all years particularly the geriatric patient should be the function of the pastoral counselor.

Admittedly such concepts are difficult to define, even more difficult to quantify and measure. This, however, should not inhibit the pastoral counselor's reaching out to the geriatric to meet the needs of the spirit. To deal only with physical and emotional needs is to neglect the whole person of any age. To minister to the total man should be the goal of all those in the helping professions. To do so presents not only a great challenge but also a great opportunity.

Chapter XIX

Religion and Wholistic Health

Increasing sophistication of medical technology has solved many medical problems, but in its wake it has created new moral and ethical ones. The dangers of a vacuum in relating to the patient as a total human being arise from both medical technology and faith healing. This chapter seeks to raise issues relevant to the theological and philosophic concepts of wholeness in relation to physical health.

The concept of treating the patient as a total human being includes the spiritual make-up of a person as well as their anatomy and physiology. Increasing sophistication of medical technology makes the blending of medicine and religion pressing and important. The possibility of maintaining basic physical processes by machinery opens the question of the very meaning of life and existence, and this question is certainly religious in nature. Other ethical and religious issues are encountered in the areas of abortion, genetic engineering, organ transplants, etc.

Coincidental with the great strides taken in the advancement of physical medicine has been a surge of interest in such things as folk medicine, pyramid power, acupuncture, and faith healing. While not suggesting any cause-effect relationship, it might seem to the casual observer that as medicine has advanced in technology people seem to need to have something more personal to believe in. While it is not the purpose of this discussion to go into an analysis of the many facets of modern life that may seem to give rise to the current interest in medico-religious thought, it is necessary to examine its historical, theological and philosophic roots.

The historical relationship of medicine and religion goes back into antiquity long before the advent of scientific medicine. As in contemporary primitive society the "shaman" performs both religious and medical rituals, and the relationship of sin and sickness is felt to be immediate and direct. In the Old Testament the Levitical priests not only conducted the worship of the Israelites, but they also were to make examinations and diagnose leprosy (Lev. 13, 14). Prophets, such as Elijah, were later called upon to heal the sick as part and proof of their prophetic office.

In the New Testament era the healing ministry of Jesus and later His Apostles dominated the pages of the Gospels and Acts. He embodies the healing power of love which cleanses men of sin and makes them whole again. All manner of physical and mental disorders are healed by Jesus' command. The paradox of Jesus' healing ministry is that He dies, by crucifixion, of physical wounds.

There are two aspects of supernatural healing that are signficant. One is that the healing is in response to faith and is thereby seen as more a spiritual than physical problem to begin with, and the other is that healing was usually immediate. These facets are important because they form the basis of expectations for persons looking for divine healing in the present age. These same two factors are in evidence, to some extent, in the performance of the medicine man or witch doctor. The healing art was clearly akin to magic in times past.

In modern times medicine has divorced itself from religion completely and instead has allied itself to scientific methodology. Whereas hospitals in the past were mainly established as the result of religious motivation, the modern medical center has a large laboratory and a small chapel.

Modern medicine and medical education, in concentrating almost exclusively on scientific concerns, has constructed its own credo: Trust the physician and his medicine.

Admittedly, these are generalizations and many exceptions can be noted. However, the current emphasis on hospital pastoral care programs and the large popular response to public services of healing can be interpreted as attempts to fill a void that medical technology has created. Scientific gadgetry - enormously powerful and effective still does not, and indeed cannot treat the "whole man." At the same time, magic and superstition are not efficacious in healing a ruptured appendix. What is called for is a theology of health that will integrate the powerful healing of faith and love with the power of medical technology.

A therapeutic blend of medicine and religion means more than having a physician who is religious or having a clergyman bless a hernia repair. It must somehow permeate the entire fabric of human life. A theology of health must have a creed that encompasses the entire spectrum of man's experience. No attempt will be made to be exhaustive, but an effort will be made to be suggestive.

Several tenets can be stated. First, a view of man is necessary that allows for the unity of body, mind and spirit. That is to say that there exists in all persons a symbiotic relationship of these factors and thus whatever affects any one of these factors will automatically influence the other two. An appreciation of the concerted effort of physician, counselor and clergyman is mandatory. Thus, neither discipline should function in a private arena, isolated from the other two. Otherwise, such fragmentation will result in only a partial healing.

A second indispensable ingredient is an acceptance that all healing is miraculous. That the body heals itself is another given. Man, as God's creation, has the potential for complete physical, mental and spiritual health. Sin, as a principle, is that which works against the best good of the person in any dimension. It is also that which makes man imperfect and incomplete. God is able and willing to negate the deleterious effects of sin in man's being.

A corollary of the acceptance of God's power to heal is the acceptance of the inevitability of human physical death. The tension and balance between these two assumptions is crucial. The healing professions must accept both simultaneously. Similarly, a tension and balance must be maintained between the proposition that, God uses the medical knowledge and technology of technicians to heal, and the proposition that God may intervene without human agency in the course of an illness to effect healing.

It seems reasonable that in time of illness a person consult a physician as a primary action. This is not a lapse of faith since physicians are trained to assist and promote the healing processes of the body. In the New Testament Luke, the gospel writer is referred to as the "beloved physician." In the Apocrypha reference is made to the worth and dignity of the physician also. This is an apparent shift from the blending of the religious and medical ministry of the Levitical priests in the Old Testament economy referred to above.

At the same time, a person should also be alert to their own resources in the healing processes and consider to what extent they can cooperate with the physician. Mention should also be made at this point of the possibility of one's own life style contributing to the onset of illness. This brings into focus some spiritual dimensions. Emotional factors such as stress, anxiety and depression can indeed lower the body's resistance to illness and disease. At the same time, smoking, overeating, lack of exercise, alcohol and drug abuse may certainly be contributing factors also.

Thus, when one consults a physician, an attitude of being a

198

partner in the healing effort is much more constructive than viewing the situation as one in which the physician only has the resources to help. At the same time, one should also consider consulting with their religious advisor to the extent that spiritual factors appear to affect the onset or continuation of medical symptoms. The body may be signalling a spiritual malady via physical dysfunction. Ideally, then, treatment should be seen in terms of meeting the needs of the whole person - body, soul and spirit.

The apparent success of faith healers certainly suggests that the spiritual resources of the person be included in most therapeutic programs. The ideal healing milieu would seem to be one in which all aspects of the individual's needs be considered. A recognition of the impact of the spiritual dimension in healing is sometimes missed by physicians who are primarily trained in scientific methodology. Religious advisors also need to appreciate the healing expertise of health professionals and seek to work in concert with them.

In this context, healing is seen as a significant, enabling work of God through human agency. Healing can always be considered miraculous, and be received thankfully. Hopefully, the healing will always be complete and permanent. However, the inevitability of human death must always be considered, as well as the possibility of chronic disease. In these instances the miracle of healing will be primarily spiritual in nature, but none the less a work of God also. The Apostle Paul prayed three times that he be delivered of a chronic disease, but was instructed that God's grace would be given in sufficient measure to enable him to endure rather than be cured. Whether the miracle be the physical healing or the grace to endure the physical condition, one's religious faith is an invaluable asset. A realistic acceptance of these alternatives, without surrendering to fatalism, will set the stage for whole and wholesome health.

Conclusion

It is difficult in a work of this nature and scope to convey adequately the importance the writer places on the often intangible elements of Scripture and prayer in the work of the pastoral counselor. Although reference has been made repeatedly concerning the efficacy of these spiritual tools, it should be noted that the personal faith of the pastoral counselor is an indispensable ingredient in the effective use of these tools in his encounters with patient and staff.

This means that the pastoral counselor must be grounded in and saturated with a mature trust in the wisdom and goodness of God. His personal belief in the Lord as the Creator and Sustainer of the universe provides the motivation and inner strength for his pastoral counseling efforts. Believing in a God who can and does intervene in the natural course of human illness and recuperation provides the basis for healing and therapeutic prayer.

A personal acceptance and appreciation for the sacrificial suffering of Christ is essential in ministering to the spiritual and physical needs of others. The pastoral counselor cannot give that which he does not himself possess. Personally accepting the love and forgiveness of God in Christ, equips the pastoral counselor to offer these freely to those he endeavors to help.

An implicit personal belief in the Scripture he uses, further enhances the pastoral counselor's effectiveness. To accept the Scripture as God's supernatural revelation to man is to believe that it can be genuinely beneficial to those who read it and hear it. Also, the healing power of the sacrament of communion is based on the faith of the one who administers it as well as those who receive it.

It is hoped that these foregoing chapters will provide the pastoral counselor with the insight and sensitivity to communicate his faith effectively to those under physical and emotional duress. Finally, it should be noted that the pastoral counselor in visiting the sick is showing compassion to Christ Himself and will be rewarded accordingly.

Appendix A

A Living Will

This is one example of a "living will." In order to make the best use of your Living Will consider the following:

1. Sign and date before two witnesses. (This is to insure that you signed of your own free will and not under any pressure.)

2. If you have a doctor, give him a copy for your medical file and discuss it with him to make sure he is in agreement.

   Give copies to those most likely to be concerned "if the time comes when you can no longer take part in decisions for your own future." Enter their names on the bottom line of the Living Will.Keep the original nearby, easily and readily available.

3. Above all discuss your intentions with those closest to you, NOW.

4. It is a good idea to look over your Living Will once a year and redate it and initial the new date to make it clear that your wishes are unchanged.

TO MY FAMILY, MY PHYSICIAN, MY LAWYER, MY CLERGYMAN
TO ANY MEDICAL FACILITY IN WHOSE CARE I HAPPEN TO BE
TO ANY INDIVIDUAL WHO MAY BECOME RESPONSIBLE FOR MY HEALTH, WELFARE OR AFFAIRS

Death is as much a reality as birth, growth, maturity and old age—it is the one certainty of life. If the time comes when I, can no longer take part in decisions for my own future, let this statement stand as an expression of my wishes, while I am still of sound mind.

If the situation should arise in which there is no reasonable expectation of my recovery from physical or mental disability, I request that I be allowed to die and not be kept alive by artificial means or "heroic measures." I do not fear death itself as much as the indignities of deterioration, dependence and hopeless pain. I, therefore, ask that medication be mercifully administered to me to alleviate suffering even though this may hasten the moment of death.

This request is made after careful consideration. I hope you who care for me will feel morally bound to follow its mandate. I recognize that this appears to place a heavy responsibility upon you, but it is with the intention of relieving you of such responsibility and of placing it upon myself in accordance with my strong convictions, that this statement is made.

Signed _____

Date _____

Witness _____

Witness _____

Copies of this request have been given to _____

_____

_____

_____

Bibliography

Anonymous, "Cancer Facts and Figures." New York: The American Cancer Society, 1975.

Anonymous, "The Clergy and the Cancer Patient." New York: The American Cancer Society, 1975.

Anonymous, "Patients' Days." *British Medical Journal*, Vol. 2, No. 6034, August 28, 1976, pp. 490.

Anonymous, "Psychological Hazards of Convalescence after Myocardial Infarction." *Lancet*. Vol. 1, 1971.

Anonymous, "Blood, Medicine and the Law of God." (pamphlet, published by Watchtower Bible and Tract Society of Pennsylvania, 1961).

Anonymous, "Self-Injury," *The Lancet*. Vol. II, October 19, 1974.

Arieti, S., editor, *American Handbook of Psychiatry*. 3 vols. (New York: Basic Books, Inc., 1959) II, 1232.

Ballinger, Malcomb B., "Religious Care for Hospital Patients," Indianapolis: Methodist Hospital of Indiana, 1969.

Barckley, Virginia, "Families Facing Cancer." *Cancer News*, Spring/Summer, 1970. New York: The American Cancer Society.

Baughman, William H., Bruha, John C., and Gould, Francis J., "Euthanasia" Criminal, Tort, Constitutional and Legislative Considerations." *Notre Dame Lawyer*. Vol. 48, No. 5, June 1973.

Bird, Brian, *Talking with Patients*. 2nd Edition. Philadelphia: J. B. Lippincott, 1973.

Boisen, Anlon T., *Out of the Depths*. New York: Harper and Brothers, 1960.

Bouchard, R., and Owens, N.F., *Nursing Care of the Cancer Patient*. St. Louis: C. V. Mosby Co., 1972. 2nd Edition.

Bowers, Margaretta K., Jackson, Edgar N., Knight, James, LeShaw, Lawrence, *Counseling the Dying*. New York: Aronson, 1975.

Brown, Helene, "Cancer Quackery: What Can You Do About It?" *Nursing 1975*, Vol. 5, May 1975.

Bruegel, M. A., "Relationship of Preoperative Anxiety to Perception of Postoperative Pain." *Nursing Research*. Vol. 20, No. 1, Jan-Feb 1971, pp. 26-31.

Burt, Margaret M., "Perceptual Deficits in Hemiplegia." *American Journal of Nursing*. Vol. 70, No. 5, May 1970, p. 1027.

Butler, Robert N., and Lewis, M. I., *Aging and Mental Health*. St. Louis: C. V. Mosby Co., 1973.

Caine, Donald, "Psychological Considerations Affecting Rehabilitation After Amputation." *The Medical Journal of Australia.* Vol. 2, October 1973.

Cassem, N. H. and Hackett, Thomas P., "Psychiatric Consultation in a Coronary Care Unit." *Annals of Internal Medicine.* Vol. 75, 1971.

Clarke-Williams, M. J., "Lower Limb Amputation in the Elderly." *Nursing Times,* December 1974.

Clinebell, Howard J., Jr., *Mental Health Through Christian Community.* New York: Abingdon Press, 1965.

Clingan, Donald F., "Insights on Aging from Research and Experience—Spiritual Insights." Presentation made at National Seminar to Educate Clergy for Service in Aging. Indianapolis, February, 1978.

Collins, Gary R., *The Christian Psychology of Paul Tournier.* Grand Rapids, Michigan: Baker Book House, 1973.

Combs, Arthur W., and Syngg, Donald, *Individual Behavior.* Revised Edition. New York: Harper and Row, 1959, pp. 161-162.

Corbus, H. F. and Connell, R. W., "The Patient's Needs—Does Anyone Care?" *Hospitals, J. A. H. A.,* Vol. 48, January 16, 1974, pp. 24 ff.

Cousins, Norman, "Anatomy of an Illness (As Perceived by the Patient)." *The New England Journal of Medicine,* Vol. 295, No. 26, December 23, 1976, pp. 1458-63.

Cratty, Bryant J., *Perceptual and Motor Developments in Infants and Children.* New York: The Macmillan Co., 1970, p. 102.

DeHaan, M. R., "Divine Healing and Divine Healers." (pamphlet, no publisher listed or publication date).

Eason, William M., *The Dying Child.* Springfield, Illinois: Charles C. Thomas, 1970.

Eckenhoff, James E., editor, *The Medical Clinics of North America.* "Pain and Its Clinical Management." Vol. 52, No. 1, January 1968. Philadelphia: W. B. Saunders Co., p. 220.

EKDDY, Mary Baker, *Science and Health with Key to the Scriptures.* Boston: First Church of Christ, Scientist, 1975.

Edwards, Griffith, & Grant, Marcus, editors, *Alcoholism - New Knowledge and New Responses.* Baltimore: University Park Press, 1977

Enelow, A. J., and Weinstein, H. M., "Uncovering Depression in the Anxious Patient." Merck and Co., Inc., 1973.

Engel, George L., and Romano, John, "Delirium, A Syndrome of Cerebral Insufficiency." *Journal of Chronic Diseases.* Vol. 9, No. 3, March 1959, p. 269.

Erikson, Eric, *Identity, Youth and Crisis.* New York: W. W. Norton, 1968.

Farrell, Jane, "Nursing Care of the Patient in a Cast Brace" *Nursing Clinics of North America.* Vol. II, No. 4, December 1976.

Finley, Mike, "Cancerophobia." *Update*. Minneapolis: University of Minnesota, Vol. 4, No. 2, Fall 1976.

Fletcher, George P., "Prolonging Life." *Washington Law Review*, Vol. 42, No. 999, 1967.

Forgus, Ronald H., *Perception. The Basic Process in Cognitive Development*. New York: McGraw-Hill, 1964, p. 161.

Foster, Sue and Andreoli, Kathleen G., "Behavior Following Acute Myocardial Infarction." *American Journal of Nursing*, Vol. 70, No. 11, November 1970.

Freedman, A. F., Kaplan, Harold I., and Sadock, Benjamin J., *Modern Synoposis of Psychiatry*. Baltimore: The Williams and Wilkins Co., 1972

Friedman, Lawrence W., "The Quality of Hope for the Amputee." *Archives of Surgery*. Vol. 110, June 1975.

Friedman, Meyer and Rosenman, R. H., *Type A, Behavior and Your Heart*. New York: Alfred A. Knopf, 1974.

Gallant, D. M., and Simpson, G., editors, *Depression: Behavioral, Biochemical, Diagnoistic and Treatment Concepts*. New York: Spectrum Publications, Inc., 1976.

Gibson, James J., *Senses Considered as Perceptual Systems*. Boston: Houghton-Mifflin Co., 1966, pp. 47-50.

Gilson, George J., "Care of the Family Who Has Lost a Newborn," *Postgraduate Medicine*, Vol. 60, No. 4, December 1976.

Graham, Lois E., and Conley, Elizabeth, "Evaluation of Anxiety and Fear in Adult Surgical Patients." *Nursing Research*, Vol. 20, No. 2, March-April 1971, pp. 113-122.

Green, Edward, and Simmons, Henry, "Toward an Understanding of the Religious Needs in Aging Persons." *The Journal of Pastoral Care*. Vol. XXXI, No. 4. December, 1977.

Groves, James E., "Taking Care of the Hateful Patient." *The New England Journal of Medicine*. Vol. 298, No. 16. April 20, 1978

Hagan, Joan M., "Infant Death: Nursing Interaction and Intervention with Grieving Families." *Nursing Forum*, Vol. 13, No. 4, 1974.

Harris, Louis and Associates, Inc. "The Myth and Reality of Aging in America." Washington: The National Council on Aging, Inc., 1975.

Heffron, Warren A., "Group Therapy Sessions As Part of Treatment of Children with Cancer." *Pediatric Annals*, February, 1975.

Heffron, Warren A., Bommelaere, Karen, and Masters, Ruth, "Group Discussions with the Parents of Leukemic Children." *Pediatrics*, Vol. 52, No. 6, December 1973.

Herzberg, Joseph, "Self-Excoriation by Young Women," *American Journal of Psychiatry*. Vol. 134, No. 3, March, 1977.

Hill, Thomas E., *Contemporary Theories of Knowledge*. New York,: The Ronald Press, 1961.

Hiltner, Seward, Editor, *Toward a Theology of Aging*. New York: Human Sciences Press, 1975.

Holleb, Arthur I., "A Patient's Right to Die. . . The Easy Way Out?" *Ca - A Cancer Journal for Clinicians*, Vol. 24, No. 4, July/August 1974.

Holst, Lawrence E., and Kurtz, Harold P., editors, *Toward a Creative Chaplaincy*. Springfield, Illinois: Charles C. Thomas, 1973.

Holy Bible. Revised Standard Version. New York: Thomas Nelson and Sons, 1952.

Hudson, Robert P., "Death, Dying, and the Zealous Phase." *Annals of Internal Medicine*, Vol. 88, No. 5, May, 1978.

Hurlock, Elizabeth, *Developmental Psychology*. New York: McGraw-Hill, Inc., 4th Edition, 1974.

Hutterer, Ilona and Denes, Zsuzsanna, "Psychosomatic Rehabilitation of Elderly Persons." *Journal of the American Geratric Society*, Vol. 23, No. 3, 1975.

Ingelfinger, F. J., "Empty Slogan for the Dying." *The New England Journal of Medicine*, Vol. 291, No. 16, October 17, 1974.

Ingles, Thelma, "St. Christopher's Hospice." *Nursing Outlook*, Vol. 22, No. 12, December 1974.

Janis, Irving L., *Psychological Stress*, "Psychoanalytic and Behavioral Studies of Surgical Patients." New York: John Wiley and Sons, 1958.

Jensen, J., and Zahourek, R., "Depression in Mothers Who Have Lost a Newborn." *Rocky Mountain Medical Journal*, Vol. 69, No. 11, November 1972.

Johnson, Jean E., Dabbs, James M., and Leventhal, Howard, "Psychosocial Factors in the Welfare of Surgical Patients." *Nursing Research*, Vol. 19, No. 1, Jan-Feb, 1970, pp. 18-29.

Johnson, M. A., *Developing the Art of Understanding*. New York: Springer Publishing Co., Inc. 1967.

Keleman, Stanley, *Living Your Dying*. New York: Random House, 1974.

Kerney, LeRoy, "Ministering to Cancer Patients." College of Chaplains Workshop Papers, 1969.

Kovarik, Joseph L., "Extraordinary Means of Postponing Death." *Rocky Mountain Medical Journal*, Vol. 71, No. 10, October 1974.

Krupp, Neal E., "Adaptation on Chronic Illness." *Postgraduate Medicine*, Vol. 60, No. 5, November 1976.

Kubler-Ross, Elizabeth, *On Death and Dying*. New York: Macmillan Publishing Co., Inc., 1969.

　　　　　Death—The Final Stage of Growth, Englewood Cliffs, N.J., Prentice-Hall, 1975.

        Questions and Answers on Death and Dying. New York: Macmillan, 1974.

        "What Is It Like To Be Dying?" *American Journal of Nursing,* Vol. 71, No. 1, January 1971.

Larson, Raymond L., "Using Psychology to Enhance Patient Care, Account Collection." *Hospital Financial Management,* Vol. 25, January 1971, pp. 46-49.

Lederer, Henry D., "How the Sick View Their World." *Journal of Social Issues,* Vol. 8, 1952, pp. 161-162

Lesse, Stanley, editor, *Masked Depression.* New York: Aronson, 1974.

Levitt, Ruth, "Attitudes of Hospital Patients." *Nursing Times,* Vol. 71, No. 13, March 27, 1975, pp. 497-499.

Lucas, M. A., "Praying with the Terminally Ill." *Hospital Progress.* Vol. 59, No. 3, March, 1978.

Maguire, David C., *Death by Choice.* Garden City, New York: Doubleday and Co., Inc. 1974.

Martin, Bernard, *The Healing Ministry in the Church.* Richmond, Virginia: John Knox Press, 1961.

Marty, Alan T., "The Pagan Roots of Western Hospital." *Surgery, Gynecology and Obstetrics,* Vol. 133, December 1961.

Mazzola, Rosanne and Jacobs, George B., "Social and Psychological Implications of Paraplegia." *Journal of Neurosurgical Nursing,* Vol. 5, No. 2, December 1973.

McCormick, Richard A., "The New Medicine and Morality." *Theology Digest,* Vol. 21, No. 4, Winter 1973.

Mead, Margaret, "The Right to Die." *Nursing Outlook,* Vol. 16, No. 10, October 1968.

Melzack, Ronald, and Wall, Patrick D., "Pain Mechanisms: A New Theory," *Science,* Vol. 150, No. 3699, November 1965, p. 974.

Mendels, Joseph, *Concepts of Depression.* New York: John Wiley and Sons, Inc., 1970.

Menninger, Karl, *Man Against Himself.* New York: Harcourt, 1938.

Miles, C. P., "Conditions Predisposing to Suicide: A Review." *The Journal of Nervous and Mental Disease.* Vol. 164, No. 4, April 1977.

Miller, James S., M.D., "Therapies Ministers Use." *The Christian Century,* Vol. XCIV, No. 19, May 25, 1977.

Milt, Harry, *Alcoholism: Its Causes and Cures.* New York: Scribners, 1976.

Nighswonger, Carl A., "Ministry to the Dying as a Learning Encounter." *Journal of Pastoral Care.* Vol. XXVI, No. 2, June, 1972.

O'Neill, Reginald, editor, *Readings in Epistemology.* New York: Irvington Publications, 1961.

Pasnau, Robert O. and Pfefferbaum, Betty, "Psychological Aspects of Post-Amputation Pain." *Nursing Clinics of North America*, Vol. 11, No. 4, December 1976.

Pfefferbaum, Betty and Pasnau, Robert O., "Post-Amputation Grief," *Nursing Clinics of North America*, Vol. 11, No. 4, December 1976.

Pike, Noreen, "In Hospital—The Adult Patient's View," *Nursing Mirror*, Vol. 140, No. 17, April 25, 1975, pp. 67-69.

Pollock, William F., " 'Cognitive' and 'Sapient'—Which Death Is the Real Death?" *The American Journal of Surgery*. Vol. 136, July, 1978.

Rachels, James, "Active and Passive Euthanasia," *The New England Journal of Medicine*, Vol. 292, No. 2, January 9, 1975.

Ramsay, M. A. E., "A Survey of Pre-operative Fear," *Anaesthesia*, Vol. 27, No. 4, October 1972, pp. 296-402.

Risley, Mary, *House of Healing - The Story of the Hospital*," Garden City, New York: Doubleday and Co., 1961.

Rosen, David H., "The Serious Suicide Attempt." *Journal of the American Medical Association*. Vol. 235, No. 19, May 10, 1976.

Rovinsky, Joseph J. and Guttmacher, Alan F., editors, *Medical, Surgical and Gynecological Complications of Pregnancy*, 2nd edition, Baltimore: The Williams and Wilkins Co., 1965.

Ruitenbeek, Hendrik M., editor, *The Interpretation of Death*. New York: Aronson, 1973.

Russell, William D., "My Baby's Dead." *The Journal of Pastoral Care*, Vol. 29, No. 3, September 1975.

Sanford, Agnes, *The Healing Gifts of the Spirit*, Philadelphia: J. B. Lippincott Co., 1966.

Saylor, Dennis E., "The Quality of Life as a Factor in Determining the Prolongation of Life." *Bulletin A. P. H. A.*, 1977 Convention Edition, Vol. XLI, No. 2.

Schuyler, Dean, *The Depressive Spectrum*. New York: Aronson, 1975

Seitz, P., and Warrick, L., "Perinatal Death: The Grieving Mother," *American Journal of Nursing*, Vol. 74, No. 11, November 1974.

Shetler, Mary G., "Operating Room Nurses Go Visiting." *American Journal of Nursing*, Vol. 72, No. 7, July 1972, pp. 1266-69.

Shneidman, Edwin J., *Suicidology: Contemporary Developments*. New York: Greene & Stratton, 1976

Shoenberg, B., Carr, Austin C., Perety, David and Kutscher, Austin H., *Loss and Grief - Psychological Management in Medical Practice*. New York: Columbia University Press, 1970.

Smith, Mary C., "Patient Responses to Being Transferred during Hospitalization." *Nursing Research*, Vol. 25, No. 3, May-June 1976, pp. 192-196.

210

Smith, William A., "Ministering to the Depressed Person." *The Journal of Pastoral Care*, Vol. XXVI, No. 1, March, 1972.

Sneddon, Ian, and Sneddon, Joan, "Self-inflicted Injury: A follow-up Study of 43 Patients." *British Medical Journal.* Vol. III, August 30, 1975.

Steger, Herbert G., "Understanding the Psychologic Factors in Rehabilitation." *Geriatrics*, May 1976.

Swanson, David W., "Less Obvious Aspects of Chronic Pain." *Postgraduate Medicine*, Vol. 60, No. 5, November 1976.

Swanson, David W., et al, "Program for Managing Chronic Pain." *Mayo Clinic Proceedings*, Vol. 51, July 1976.

Tyzenhouse, Phyllis, "Myocardial Infarction: Its Effect on the Family." *American Journal of Nursing*, Vol. 73, No. 6, June 1973.

Vanderpool, Harold Y., "The Ethics of Terminal Care." *Journal of the American Medical Association.* Vol. 239, No. 9, February 27, 1978.

Vaughn, N. L., "The Right to Die." *California Western Law Review*, Vol. 10, 1974.

Veach, Robert M., "The Whole Brain Oriented Concept of Death: An Outmoded Philosophical Formulation." *Journal of Thanotology*, Vol. 3, No. 1, 1975.

Vollicer, Beverly J., "Perceived Stress Level of Events Associated with the Experience of Hospitalization." *Nursing Research*, Vol. 22, No. 6, November-December 1973.

von Fieandt, K., *The World of Perception.* Homewood, Illinois: The Dorsey Press, 1966, p. 65.

Weikel, William, et al, "Counselors and Clergy: Why Not Teamwork?" *Journal of Rehabilitation*, Vol. 40, No. 4, July/August, 1974.

Williams, Florence, "The Crisis of Hospitalization." *Nursing Clinics of North America*, Vol. 9, No. 1, March 1974, pp. 37-45.

Williams, James, Jones, John R., and Williams, Barbara, "A Physiological Measure of Pre-operative Anxiety." *Psychosomatic Medicine*, Vol. 31, No. 6, 1969, pp. 522-527.

Williams, Rosemary, "Handling Anxiety." *Nursing '73*, Vol. 3, No. 9, September 1973, p. 25.

Winslow, Elizabeth H., and Fuhs, Margaret F., "Preoperative Assessment for Postoperative Evaluation." *American Journal of Nursing*, Vol. 73, No. 8, August 1973, pp. 1372-74.

Wilson, William P., et al, "Observations on Pain and Suffering." *Psychosomatics*, Vol. 17, April-June 1976.

Wolfer, John, and Davis, Carol E., "Assessment of Surgical Patients: Preoperative Emotional Condition and Postoperative Welfare." *Nursing Research*, Vol. 19, No. 5, September-October 1970, pp. 403-414.

211

Wrzesniewski, K., "The Attitudes Toward the Illness of Patients After Myocardial Infarction Undergoing Rehabilitation." *Social Science and Medicine*, Vol. 9, No. 4-5, April-May 1975.

Zahourek, R., and Jensen, J. S., "Grieving and the Loss of the Newborn." *American Journal of Nursing*, Vol. 73, No. 5, May 1973.

Zimring, Joseph G., "The Right to Die with Dignity." *New York State Journal of Medicine*, Vol. 73, July 1973.

212